HUMAN RESOURCES GUIDES FROM LEXISNEXIS

$120 Looseleaf Binder w/ CD-ROM, 586 pages
ISBN 0327018623

EMPLOYMENT FORMS AND POLICIES, 4th Ed., with CD-ROM

by Maureen F. Moore

Save time and avoid legal hassles with this comprehensive guide containing more than 300 forms, policies and checklists covering:

- Hiring and Selection
- New Employees
- Payroll Issues
- Leaves and Benefits
- Performance Appraisals
- Terminations
- and much more!

Employment law attorney Maureen F. Moore provides expert commentary and suggestions which will leave you fully prepared to handle everything from casual day dress codes to workplace violence policies.

OCCUPATIONAL SAFETY AND HEALTH HANDBOOK: An Employer's Guide, 2nd Ed.

by Jeffrey L. Hirsch

Avoid costly penalties for OSHA violations and manage your company's safety and health risks with this clearly written desktop guide.

$115 Looseleaf Binder, 700 pages
ISBN 0327001984

EMPLOYER'S GUIDE TO DISCRIMINATION LAW, 1st Ed.

by Maureen F. Moore

This concise guide explains the essential facts employers need to know about race, sex, age, disability, and other types of discrimination. Includes a CD-ROM with employment forms and training slides.

$28 softcover w/ CD-ROM, 285 pages
ISBN: 0820599867

SUPERVISOR'S GUIDE TO EMPLOYEE PERFORMANCE REVIEWS, 4th Ed.

by Mike Deblieux & Lee T. Paterson

A step-by-step guide to effective performance reviews, with sample forms and instructions.

$36 Softbound, 134 pages, ISBN 0820597864

ADA COMPLIANCE MANUAL FOR EMPLOYERS, 2nd Ed.

by Maureen F. Moore

Comprehensive coverage of the Americans with Disabilities Act. Practical information at every phase of the employment relationship, from establishing job requirements to reducing termination risks.

$95 Looseleaf Binder, 748 pages
ISBN: 0327103183

DOCUMENTING EMPLOYEE DISCIPLINE, 4th Ed.

by Lee T. Paterson & Mike Deblieux

Learn how to use documentation to improve employee performance and prevent unnecessary lawsuits.

$46 Softbound, 189 pages, ISBN 0820597872

SUPERVISOR'S GUIDE TO DOCUMENTING EMPLOYEE DISCIPLINE, 5th Ed.

by Lee T. Paterson & Mike Deblieux

This abridged version of **Documenting Employee Discipline** helps front-line supervisors motivate employees while avoiding unnecessary lawsuits.

$27 Softbound, 90 pages, ISBN 0820597856

LexisNexis™

Phone 800-533-1637
Fax 800 828-8341
Online www.lexisnexis.com/bookstore

Pre-Employment Screening From LexisNexis
LexisNexis, the leading provider of information-driven services now offers a comprehensive pre-employment screening solution:
PEOPLEWISE
PeopleWise combines the speed of the Internet with the power of LexisNexis services to help you:
• Accelerate hiring decisions.
• Ensure compliance with the Fair Credit Reporting Act.
• Reduce overall screening costs.
Visit the PeopleWise Recruiting and Staffing Corner on the Workforce website at www.workforce.com/peoplewise.
LexisNexis PeopleWise
For information about PeopleWise, call: 1-877-447-9473
LEXIS and NEXIS are registered trademarks of Reed Elsevier Properties Inc., used under license. PeopleWise is a registered trademark of PeopleWise, LLC., and the LexisNexis PeopleWise logo is a trademark of LexisNexis. © 2003 LEXIS-NEXIS, a division of Reed Elsevier, Inc. All rights reserved.

LEGAL THRILLERS!
GRIPPING PAGE-TURNERS!!
You won't find any fictional courtroom dramas at our bookstore, or for that matter the latest tale of legal suspense. But if you're searching for gripping page-turners by the real masters of legal intrigue, go to the LexisNexis™ Bookstore at www.lexisnexis.com/bookstore. You'll find the classics – from Matthew Bender®, Michie™ and *Shepard's*® – all expertly done, packed with authentic detail, and highly readable. Pick up one of our captivating legal thrillers today.
Save 10% when you shop www.lexisnexis.com/bookstore for Matthew Bender, Michie or *Shepard's* products. Use code AD115 at checkout.
LexisNexis™
It's how you know™
LexisNexis, the Knowledge Burst logo, and Michie are trademarks and *Shepard's* is a registered trademark of Reed Elsevier Properties Inc., used under license. Matthew Bender is a registered trademark of Matthew Bender Properties Inc. It's How You Know is a trademark of LexisNexis, a division of Reed Elsevier Inc.
© 2003 LexisNexis, a division of Reed Elsevier Inc. All rights reserved.

INVESTIGATING EMPLOYEE COMPLAINTS

How to Handle Harassment, Favoritism, Performance, Theft, and Other Problems

First Edition

by

Maureen Moore
Lynn Pham Moore & Ross, P.C.
Dallas, Texas

LexisNexis®

QUESTIONS ABOUT THIS PUBLICATION?

For CUSTOMER SERVICE ASSISTANCE concerning replacement pages, shipments, billing, reprint permission, or other matters,

please call Customer Service Department at 800-833-9844
email *customer.support@lexisnexis.com*
or visit our interactive customer service website at *www.lexisnexis.com/printcdsc*

For EDITORIAL **content questions** concerning this publication,

please call 800-446-3410 ext. 7447
or email: *LLP.CLP@lexisnexis.com*

For **information on other LEXISNEXIS MATTHEW BENDER publications,**

please call us at 800-223-1940
or visit our online bookstore at *www.lexisnexis.com/bookstore*

ISBN: 0-8205-8645-5

LexisNexis®

Matthew Bender & Company, Inc.
Editorial Offices
P.O. Box 7587
Charlottesville, VA 22906-7587
800-446-3410
www.lexisnexis.com

PRINTED WITH SOY INK™

Product Number 2262010

(Pub. 22620)

ABOUT THE AUTHOR

Maureen Moore, a partner with Lynn Pham Moore & Ross, P.C., in Dallas, Texas, has specialized in the practice of labor and employment law on the management side for more than twenty years. She has considerable experience with all facets of the employment relationship on local, national, and international levels.

Ms. Moore is licensed to practice in Texas and various federal courts across the country, and is Board Certified in Labor and Employment Law by the Texas Board of Legal Specialization. Her practice includes labor and employment litigation, arbitration, OSHA inspections, OFCCP and discrimination complaints, remaining union-free, collective bargaining, corporate employment policies, and general counseling on personnel and employment policies.

Ms. Moore advises, lectures, and conducts training sessions on many topics affecting the employment relationship. She is a frequent guest speaker on topics such as the Americans with Disabilities Act, protecting yourself and your company from liability, the Family and Medical Leave Act, and employment law updates. She is a member of the ADA Compliance Group, a charter member of the Board of Advisors for the National Association for Alternative Staffing, and a certified mediator and member of the American Arbitration Association Employment Mediation and Arbitration panel.

Ms. Moore publishes frequently on many employment issues. She has also authored *The ADA Compliance Manual for Employers, Employer's Guide to Discrimination Law*, and *Employment Forms and Policies*, also published by LexisNexis®.

TABLE OF CONTENTS

TABLE OF FORMS AND POLICIES

CHAPTER 1

WHY EFFECTIVE INVESTIGATIONS ARE IMPORTANT

Dispute resolution and litigation avoidance. These are the principal reasons it is important that you conduct effective investigations of workplace complaints. Unfortunately, in today's extremely litigious society, litigation has become very expensive and a waste of time and resources. By conducting effective investigations you may be able to either avoid litigation in its entirety, or cut short any litigation that does ensue by resolving your employee disputes without involving third parties or effectively insulating yourself from legal liability. It is much more efficient, and less expensive, to resolve matters with an internal complaint process instead of with a lawsuit.

Developing appropriate investigative skills may also be necessary to satisfy legal obligations that exist under applicable law, such as to investigate complaints of harassment. Or you may be contractually required to investigate any employee complaints. In either case, it is important that the individual conducting the investigation know how to investigate workplace issues.

The type of litigation in which you may get involved may concern not only the employee with the complaint, but also the employee who was the focus of the investigation. Although not actionable in most states, some courts actually recognize a cause of action brought against an employer by a terminated employee for conducting the investigation in a negligent manner. Even if you operate in states that do not recognize such a claim, remember that bad facts make bad law. Many of the cases expanding the rights of employees to sue involve employers who engaged in outrageous actions then sought to defend those actions under the laws in existence at the time. These types of outrageous fact patterns are the ones that invite some courts to create new causes of action or expand ones that already exist. You can avoid your company's name being associated with a new cause of action relating to investigations if you learn how to, and actually conduct, effective investigations of employee complaints. It is no less expensive to be sued by the target of the investigation as opposed to the complainant, so it is best to seek to avoid both types of litigation.

The early cases involving investigations of employee actions usually involved sexual harassment complaints. Since harassment actions can exist with respect to any type of protected activity, however, the scope of investigations expanded as the law recognized these additional types of harassment claims. And as courts and employees became more familiar with the concept of investigations, they expected employers to conduct investigations whenever there was an employee dispute. Now, it is important to investigate significant complaints where there are genuine issues of material fact. These situations can involve all types of employment actions and result in all types of disciplinary action. They may also result in discrimination or wrongful discharge claims when the target is, or is not, disciplined. Since conducting investigations has become a regular requirement of Human Resource departments, the better you and your staff are at conducting investigations, the more credibility you will have with your employees and the more willing they will be to resolve disputes through your internal system.

Although it is important to understand what legal actions may stem from investigations or their results, conducting an effective investigation is more about details than application of the law. While the devil is indeed in the details in investigations, paying attention to those details and sharpening your skills in collecting and interpreting facts, will be your best defense when justifying the scope and results of your investigations.

Judges, arbitrators, and juries will evaluate what an employer knew and what the employer should have known when reviewing complaints of, and actions taken against, employees. Deficiencies in investigations may be fatal to upholding disciplinary action, whether taken against the complainant or the target of the investigation. Some employers believe the passage of time will make complaints go away and will seek to delay an investigation. Others do not conduct investigations because they are afraid of getting sued by the employee who should be investigated. It is necessary to defeat these mindsets in order to conduct investigations that will be viewed as effective and to take necessary actions.

You may be concerned about the burden of proof when conducting an investigation. Employer investigations are not criminal matters and do not require that a certain level of proof be met in order to make a recommendation. The standard applied to determine if employer investigations are sufficient is one of good faith. If you conducted a thorough investigation and reached a good faith conclusion, there should be no liability even if that good faith conclusion turns out to be incorrect. Therefore, your goal when conducting an investigation is to do all that is necessary to reach a reasonable conclusion. Investigative deficiencies are generally fatal only when there is a material effect on the fact finding process that affected the employer's disciplinary decision.

Throughout this book, recommendations will be made on how to conduct your investigation. Chapter 12 contains a training case study, questions for you to answer, and recommends answers or courses of action designed to help you hone your investigative skills and understand different ways to conduct an investigation. It also contains a presentation that can be used to train others who will be conducting investigations or to familiarize managers and supervisors with the process of conducting investigations. Before conducting an investigation, however, you need to know what can trigger the need for one. Not all employee complaints require an investigation and in order to conserve your resources, you must be able to recognize when an investigation is warranted.

CHAPTER 2

WHAT MAY TRIGGER THE NEED FOR AN INVESTIGATION

There are four general situations that may trigger the need to conduct an investigation. By far, the most common way is for an employee to complain about a co-worker, supervisor, manager or third party on your premises. Employees, however, do not always make complaints in the same manner. While some employees will follow the procedure set forth in your handbook or policy manual, others may be more circumspect about their complaints. Some will couch them in vague terms or indicate it is another employee who is having the problem. Others will confide in a supervisor with whom they have a special relationship, but will ask the supervisor to keep the matter confidential and not take any action. Employees who complain but then ask that nothing be done cannot stop the company from conducting an investigation when necessary. Regardless of what conditions an employee may place on making the complaint, a jury will consider the employer to have been put on notice of the problem once it receives sufficient knowledge to know a problem may exist. Therefore, even a confidential complaint may require that an investigation be conducted.

Employees being terminated or subject to disciplinary action may also make a complaint at the time the discipline is issued. Although you may be inclined to conclude that the employee who complains only at this time is making a false complaint just to avoid the imposition of disciplinary action, the complaint still may require an investigation. For example, if a female employee complains of sexual harassment at the time of her termination yet you do not conduct any investigation, if it turns out that the manager has been harassing employees, your failure to conduct an investigation when the first complaint was received at the female's termination may result in liability against your company for later similar complaints against the same manager. It is important to be able to identify and recognize your obligation to investigate whenever an employee makes a complaint.

Employees may also complain that other employees are being subjected to harassing or otherwise unlawful treatment. Your policy on harassment should indicate that employees are to report any harassing behavior they observe, not just behavior to which they are subjected. When employees report things they observe in the workplace, you should take those equally as seriously as complaints you take from alleged victims.

The second area from which complaints may come are third parties who are in your workplace, such as customers, vendors, or contractors. Some employers hate to investigate these types of complaints because they do not want to involve the third party, particularly if it is a customer. But, if a customer has taken the time to complain to the employer, the customer clearly thinks the situation is serious enough for intervention. And, again, if a jury learns of a third-party complaint that was ignored, it may still find the employer had knowledge of the complaint and unlawfully failed to act. Therefore, third-party complaints should not be ignored.

Both employee and third-party complaints may be made anonymously. In the past, many employers ignored such complaints requiring the employee or third party to identify himself or herself before any investigation would be conducted. Just because a complaint is made anonymously does not mean that it has no merit. In cases involving a senior executive, an employee may be so fearful of the executive that the employee fears identifying himself or herself when making the complaint. While conducting an investigation based upon an anonymous complaint may be more difficult because of the inability to talk to the complainant, an investigation may still be warranted.

Pursuant to the Sarbanes Oxley Act of 2002, public companies are required to set up methods for anonymous complaints about financial improprieties to be made. Unfortunately, there is no way to ensure that only financial complaints will be made. If you have such a system, you can be assured that employees will use whatever method you have set up to make other types of complaints about the workplace. It is important that you not only comply with the Sarbanes-Oxley requirements, but that you also have a method for ensuring that employment complaints received are forwarded to Human Resources for a determination if additional action is warranted.

Annual policy, compensation, performance, or statistical reviews may also highlight the need for an investigation. For example, if a supervisor suddenly has performance issues with all the females in his department, that may indicate something is very wrong. Or if it appears that males in a department are all receiving lower raises than females without support in the performance reviews, it may be necessary to investigate what is happening. These types of situations are far less common than direct complaints, but you must be aware that they may occur.

The final situation that can trigger the need for an investigation involves extreme changes in an employee's behavior that seem to be unexplained. This situation arises most often when drug or alcohol use or abuse in the workplace is suspected. For example, an employee who seems to be spaced out while at work, does not concentrate as well as he did before, and whose behavior is rather erratic, may make others suspect drug use. In that case, you may want to apply your drug testing policy as part of the investigation.

While these situations are the different ones that can trigger an investigation, not all of them always require that an investigation be conducted. Once a complaint is made, or situation identified, it is up to you to determine whether an investigation or any further inquiry is warranted.

CHAPTER 3

HOW TO DETERMINE WHEN AN INVESTIGATION IS WARRANTED

Not all complaints require that an investigation be conducted. Many times an employee's complaint can be resolved by explaining the company policy, correcting incorrect information, or by listening to an employee. The key is to determine if you need more facts than the employee can provide before reaching a decision. Investigations are necessary only when there are factual disputes. When an employee comes to you with a problem or complaint, one of your most important tasks will be to determine if additional information must be gathered in order to address the employee's concerns. Like a doctor evaluating a patient's recitation of symptoms, you need to determine which complaints warrant further attention. If no additional information is needed, it is not necessary to conduct an investigation.

By definition, to investigate is "to search into so as to learn the facts; inquire into systematically."[1] Investigating requires that you collect facts from other sources in a logical manner in order to reach a good faith conclusion.

When an employee comes to you with a problem, you must be able to demonstrate to the employee that you are serious, either by providing an explanation, solving the problem, or indicating an investigation will be conducted. You should ask yourself several questions in order to identify the nature of the issue and to determine what the appropriate course of action is, including: whether more facts are needed; is the issue simple or complex; are other employees involved in the situation; is just one incident involved or is a pattern emerging; and how significant is the issue. Only after you have answered these questions will you be able to determine what your next step will be.

---

1. Webster's New World College Dictionary 710 (3d ed. 1997).

In determining whether additional information is needed, you should consider whether facts from many different sources could help including witness interviews, document examination, assistance from experts, and other information that would be helpful. The witnesses may include co-workers, management or third parties who are in your workplace. It will definitely be necessary to interview witnesses if the employee indicates that other employees are involved in the situation or witnesses the incident in question.

The documents to review may include company policies, personnel files, and, probably most importantly, e-mails. If the issue is complex, it may require you to review various documents to determine what happened and if company policy was properly followed. Comparing documents may also be necessary, such as when performance reviews are involved. If the issue is of major significance to your organization, it may be necessary to review all your policies and procedures to see if the situation is covered or if you are lacking necessary procedures.

You should also ask the employee for any documentation he or she may have. Be careful, however, not to use legalistic descriptions such as documents or evidence as the employee may not interpret the term the same way you do. Instead, try to use descriptive terms such as written notes, diaries, journals, calendars, cartoons, articles, papers, manuals, policies, procedures, or e-mails.

Most employees do not think they are creating a document trail when they send and receive e-mails. And others believe all sins are forgiven if they put a note on the e-mail to "read and delete." As many now know, e-mails are never completely deleted. It is possible to recover deleted e-mails from computer hard drives, much to the chagrin of many employees and supervisors. Depending upon the nature of the complaint, you may want to ask the employee if there are old e-mails that may assist you in determining what happened.

The experts from whom you might think you can get assistance may include your in-house legal, risk management or security departments; outside legal counsel; computer experts; or accountants and auditors. The type of individuals who may provide assistance will depend upon the nature of the complaint and the type of information you are trying to collect or interpret.

Finally, as we all learned from Bill Clinton, there may be other items, such as a blue dress, which provide additional facts that help you to reach a conclusion. If you believe there are other nondocumentary items that you will need, that may indicate the necessity of conducting an investigation.

Once you have made an initial determination that some type of investigation is warranted, it is time to gather as much information as necessary from the complainant.

CHAPTER 4

THE INITIAL INTERVIEW

When the initial interview with a complainant occurs may not be within your control. An employee may come to you with a complaint that you immediately recognize will require an investigation. At that time, you may have the interview that constitutes the beginning of the investigation. Or, you may need to review a few documents before deciding if an investigation is necessary. Another situation that is common is that the employee makes a complaint at the end of the shift and needs to leave. In the latter two situations, you will have some control over when the initial interview occurs. In any event, you should also be prepared to gather the relevant information from the complainant at any time. Those who learn how to conduct effective investigations will feel comfortable beginning the investigation with or without advance notice.

A. Setting the tone

Your first task when conducting the initial interview is to set the tone and make sure the employee is comfortable talking to you and has confidence in the system. The simplest and most straightforward way of accomplishing this task is to ask the employee "is there any reason why you feel I cannot be fair and objective in resolving this matter for you?" Ninety-nine percent of the time the employee will answer that no reason exists. This response is especially true if the employee came to you in the first place. If the employee is comfortable with your objectivity, the employee already has some sense of confidence in the system.

But what if the employee admits he or she does not think you can be fair and objective? It is human nature when faced with such a statement to either argue with the individual or list the attributes that make you the perfect investigator. If you push too hard, and the employee finally relents, you may be subject to a complaint of bias or overreaching after the investigation is complete. It is acceptable to ask, "Why not?" to see if there is a simple explanation that would overcome the employee's concerns. Be careful, though, that when an employee indicates that since you are different, whether on the basis of race, sex, or other protected class, you do not respond that you can understand exactly how they feel — because you cannot. Moreover, such a statement may only reinforce the employee's perception that you cannot be objective. What you need to do is exercise your creativity to find a way to work with the employee who is making the complaint without scaring him away.

Sometimes the individual about whom the employee is complaining is so high up in the organization that the employee believes no one can be fair and objective without putting his or her job at risk. This is especially true if the complaint is leveled against the head of the organization. In such cases, it may be necessary to hire an outside agency in order to ensure employees' comfort with the process. There are many companies, comprised of former employment lawyers and human resource professionals, who offer such services. Although it is clearly more expensive to use outsiders, it may be necessary to ensure you collect all necessary facts.

Even if the target of the investigation is not someone who has power over your position, an employee may still be uncomfortable with you being the investigator. It is okay to ask an employee to recommend an appropriate investigator, so long as it is made clear that the company will make the final decision as to who the investigator will be. Sometimes the answer to your question as to why the employee does not believe you can be fair and impartial will provide enough information for you to identify someone in your organization with whom the employee would be comfortable.

If you do not instill confidence in the investigator and the process at the beginning of the investigation, you risk that the employee will take the complaint elsewhere — to a federal agency, a lawyer, other employees, or a union organizer. Therefore, put your personal feelings aside and be willing to appoint another investigator if that is what is necessary to keep the investigation on track and to resolve the complaint internally.

Once the tone is set, it is important not to ruin it with questions or statements trying to impart how serious you consider the matter to be. Opening the interview with "do you know how serious this is?" will immediately put the employee on the defensive. Regardless of how serious you think it is, the employee's view probably is that it is more serious than even you think it is, or the employee would not have found it necessary to come to you. You should also avoid comments like "are you sure you want to do this?" as that will also scare the employee away. Remember, your goal is to resolve the problem internally and to try to avoid any litigation. Scaring away the complainant will ensure you do not accomplish these goals.

There are two rules that generally apply whenever dealing with employees and they are just as important here. The first is to treat employees like you want to be treated. Put yourself in the employee's place and consider how you would expect to be treated if you were making a complaint. Second, decisions should be job related. Focus on how the employee's terms and conditions of work are affected and do not attack the employee personally. If you follow these rules, both the complainant and others will continue to have confidence in you and in the system.

B. Identifying the real issue

Unfortunately, those who complain do not present their complaints in nice, neat packages with the issues and facts identified for you. It is your job to elicit information from the individual from which you can determine what the issue is. For instance, an employee may be complaining about not getting as much overtime as in the past. After asking questions, you might learn that the supervisor was accused of making a racial statement and since that time has been giving more overtime to white employees. The complaint is not just about overtime, it is about race discrimination as well.

You probably will have already asked some questions along the lines of identifying the issues when you were determining whether it was necessary to conduct an investigation. Now is the time to flesh out what the issue really is in order to determine the scope of the investigation you need to conduct.

As many of our mothers told us — you were given two ears and one mouth so you should listen twice as much as you talk. This is good advice during an investigation. Your job is to collect information, not to offer it. It is very important that you listen to what the employee is saying and explore open items.

How do you know whether you have covered all the bases? You should take notes. These notes will help you confirm the scope of the investigation and will help to refresh your recollection of what occurred at the end of the investigation and if any litigation follows.

Instead of taking notes, some investigators like to have a witness present to take notes or use a tape recorder for all interviews. Having a witness present can stifle an employee, especially if the employee does not have the same confidence in your witness as the employee has in you or if the employee feels that the company is ganging up on her by having two people present. Using a tape recorder can also have the effect of making an employee reluctant to be candid and make him focus on the recorder and not on you. While you can use either technique, you should be aware of the inherent limitations you might be creating. And, a jury or arbitrator might read another person's notes and reach a conclusion different from what you perceived occurred. Or, a jury could reach different conclusions from listening to the tape based on vocal inflections. Since these different interpretations might result in a third party judging credibility differently than you did, they can create additional problems during litigation. *See* Chapter 6, Section F. Assessing credibility, on page 56.

C. "Just the facts, ma'am"

As Joe Friday used to say, you want "just the facts." And the best way to get the facts are by using the five W's—what, who, where, when, and why. You want to know exactly *what* happened, *who* was involved, *where* it occurred, *when* it occurred, and *why*. You will again want to know *why*. Finally, you will ask *why*.

When framing your questions, you want to avoid ones that can be answered "yes" or "no." If the employee can answer either "yes" or "no," the facts are coming from you, not from the employee. You should also avoid legalese type questions. Remember, courtroom dramas bear little resemblance to what actually occurs in a courtroom. Do not ask what evidence or proof the employee has. Nor should you ask who the witnesses are. Rather, ask if the employee has any papers, notes, expense reports, or similar things about the incident. Ask who was around when the incident occurred. Ask the employee to describe how the employee's job has been affected. Ask if this has happened before. Ask if it has happened to other employees. Ask if other employees have the same problem.

As the individual answers the questions, you will think of more questions to ask. You should leave no factual stone unturned. Follow up and do not let the employee shrink away from telling you what happened. Employees who are reluctant to provide details initially, will usually talk more openly the more they get comfortable with you. In such cases, it is important to take as much time as necessary and not try to rush the employee. Investigators who think they are surreptitiously looking at their watches, accomplish little more than telegraphing to the employee that they do not think the complaint is worth the time necessary to find out what it is.

During the course of the interview, the interviewee may attribute certain actions to others. It is important to ask the interviewee why he thinks the other person acted that way. The reason you ask *why* so often is because an individual's perception of what causes an action may lead you to discover the true underlying complaint and what actually happened.

You should also ask the employee if she talked to anyone else in the company about the problem. The answer to this question can be very significant in judging the employee's credibility. When Anita Hill accused Clarence Thomas of harassment, one of the big credibility hurdles she could not overcome in many minds was that she did not talk to anyone she logically should have discussed the issue with at the time it occurred.

One of the most common problem untrained interviewers have is letting the interviewee take control of the question. If you try to use shorthand ways of describing things, you risk the employee's interpretation of what you mean get in the way of gathering all the facts. For example, you may have a female employee who was forced to engage in sexual intercourse with a supervisor, but the employee is embarrassed about describing what happened and is hoping you will just figure it out. If you ask, "was it a problem like Monica Lewinsky had with Bill Clinton?" the employee might believe that President Clinton was right when he said that behavior was not "sex" so she answers "no, it was nothing like that." You may then believe there was no sexual contact of any type and you abandon that line of questioning. Do not let your perceptions of things lead you to try to find a different way to state what you think happened.

Even the best interviewers may not get all the relevant facts from an employee during the first interview. In order to make sure the employee has told you everything on her mind, you should ask, at the end of your inquiries, if there is anything else the employee thinks you need to know. You should also ask the employee if there are any other issues that the employee wants to discuss. While some will groan that this only invites complainers to waste more time, it makes sure that everything is out in the open and that you are not missing anything. Although time consuming, it is far less time consuming and less expensive than being involved in several years of litigation.

D. To sum it up

After you have gathered all the facts the employee can provide at that time, you need to sum up what has occurred and set the tone for the investigation to follow and ensure the employee has not lost confidence in either you or the system during the interview. First, it is important to thank the employee for bringing the matter to your attention and to remind the employee that the company does not permit retaliation against employees who raise legitimate issues. Fear of retaliation is the primary reason employees are reluctant to complain. If you ensure there is no retaliation, employees will become more comfortable with your internal process and will be more willing to use it when problems arise. It is important, however, to focus on legitimate complaints so that you preserve your right to discipline employees who make frivolous or false complaints.

If you have determined that an investigation is warranted, let the employee know that the matter will be investigated and who will be doing the investigation. In ninety-nine percent of the cases, you will be the one conducting the investigation. In some cases, however, if you are heading out of town or going on leave, it may be necessary to have someone else continue the investigation in order to prevent a long delay. If the investigator will be someone other than you, you should ensure the employee does not believe that individual is incapable of being fair or impartial. While the employee may be comfortable with you, if he is not equally comfortable with an additional investigator, the employee's confidence in the system may be destroyed.

This is a good time to briefly summarize the facts the employee gave you, the individuals identified as potential witnesses, and the documents the employee identified. If the employee has indicated she has some documentary evidence, you should agree upon a date and time when the employee will provide those documents to you. This summation gives the employee an opportunity to add any last-minute information.

It is not unusual for an employee to ask if the information provided will be kept confidential. To an employee, this usually means no one, including the target of the investigation, will be told about the complaint. You should never agree to keep something "secret" or "confidential" without an explanation. Because it will be necessary to share information obtained during the investigation, you should tell the employee that information will be shared only with those who have a legitimate, or business, need to know about what is going on.

This is a perfect time to inform the employee that you expect the employee to limit conversations about the complaint and interview to you and other investigators. You should also inform the employee that all individuals involved in the investigation will be told the same thing and will be expected to limit discussions about the investigation. If a manager is involved in the investigation, either as a target or a witness, the manager should also be reminded about the company policy against retaliation to ensure no one is threatened or subject to adverse action in order to prevent the employee from participating in the investigation or in order to force the employee to provide false information. Some employers have employees involved in the investigation sign a confidentiality form, similar to the one that follows:

CONFIDENTIALITY OF INVESTIGATION

I understand that my recent conversation with ____________________________ is part of an ongoing investigation being conducted by the Company. I further understand that I am not to discuss my conversation or any aspect of the investigation with anyone other than ____________________________. I understand that if I do engage in such discussions, I will be subject to disciplinary action, up to and including discharge.

[For management employees, add the following]

I further understand that Company policy prohibits retaliation against employees who make complaints or participate in investigations. If it is determined that I attempted to or retaliated against any individual for making a complaint or participating in an investigation, or seek to sway the information provided by anyone in an investigation, I will be subject to disciplinary action, up to and including discharge.

Employee Signature: ____

Date: ____

You will also want to ensure continued cooperation by the complainant. Some employees assume once they make the complaint they need not have any further dealings with the investigator. The employee should be informed that it may be necessary to talk to her again to gather additional information or to clarify certain things. The employee should understand that failure to cooperate might prohibit you from reaching a resolution.

You should not let the employee believe that if the investigation shows the employee is right, that the employee gets to determine what action, if any, is to be taken. Therefore, you should never promise any particular results. While you can ask the employee what may resolve the issue, you should ensure the employee understands the company will make the final decision, but the employee's input is valuable. The last thing you want is an employee to think she will make the decision and then have her recommend castration for someone who she says touched her inappropriately.

The employee will want to know when this matter will be resolved. You should not make any promises, other than to indicate that you will conduct the investigation as quickly as possible. In any event, you should not wait more than a few days before continuing the investigation.

E. When the employee asks you not to do anything

It is not uncommon, either at the beginning or at the end of an initial interview, for an employee to decide not to follow through on the complaint. The employee may ask you not to do anything, or to let the employee handle it without your assistance. It is possible that just knowing about the complaint triggers a legal obligation for the company that will require it to be investigated. You must firmly, but gently explain this fact to the employee and that you will conduct an investigation. It may be worth reminding the employee that retaliation will not be tolerated and that only those with a need to know will be told anything about the investigation.

You should try to get the employee as comfortable as you can with the fact that you now have an obligation to find out what is happening.

If the employee asks for time to handle the problem by herself, you can provide a limited period of time for her to do that before beginning your investigation. The employee should understand, however, that not much time will be allowed and if the matter is not resolved, you will go forward to find out what happened. Again, you can remind the employee of the company's policy against retaliation.

F. To document or not to document?

While many human resource professionals will tell you to document, document, document, this is one case in which whether to do so will depend upon the facts. There are two different documents that you will find some trainers strongly recommend be used in each and every investigation. In some cases, however, these documents are overkill and will only create more work for you and the complainant. In others, they may help demonstrate that you conducted a thorough and complete investigation based upon the information you had at the time.

The first document is an employee statement about the complaint, with the facts and witnesses identified. If the issue is very complex with lots of different facts and witnesses involved, it may be wise to have the employee take the time away from work to concentrate on reducing these items to writing. You run the risk, however, of having the employee think you were not listening very well if she now has to write down everything you were just told. And, depending upon the literacy of the employee, such a document may not be helpful or may only create confusion.

If, however, the employee is one whose story keeps changing or who tends to exaggerate and expand each time you talk to him, you may want to use this document to pin down the employee, in his own hand, as to what the complaints and facts are. You can also use this document as a roadmap to any additional documents the employee is going to provide, allowing him to explain the significance of the documents he gives to you.

In the event you decide it is desirable to have an employee-generated statement, you should explain to the employee that the purpose is to avoid any misunderstandings, not to create an obstacle for the employee. You should also indicate that whether to write the statement or not is entirely up to the employee and that you will not draw any conclusions, one way or the other, if the employee decides not to write the statement and is happy with your summation of what you have been told. Finally, you need to obtain an agreement as the deadline for the employee to provide the statement. You do not want to risk delaying the investigation for several weeks waiting for the employee's statement.

You should also reach agreement with the employee as to what the statement will provide. It should include a list of the employee's complaints or problems; the facts, including dates, the employee believes supports the complaints or problems; any individuals who can provide information about the complaints or problems; and identification of documents and other items the employee thinks would be helpful to making a decision, including any documents the employee has. The employee should also sign and date the statement when it is turned in to the company. It is important that the employee understand what type of information is needed, lest you risk getting a rambling, incomprehensible statement that is not helpful in planning your investigation. An example of a form you can provide for employees to complete follows:

EMPLOYEE COMPLAINT FORM

All information provided during the course of any investigation of your complaint will be kept confidential, to the extent possible. That means information will be shared only with those who have a need to know or who can assist in the investigation. No action will be taken against individuals who lodge good faith complaints of harassment. The Company depends upon your providing truthful and accurate information to allow it to conduct a full and fair investigation.

Name of employee making complaint: ______________________________

Employee(s) against whom complaint is made: ____________________

Please describe in your own words what happened, noting the date, times, and location of each incident when possible:

Was anyone around when any of these actions took place? ___ No ___ Yes

If yes, please identify each person who was there and what she or he might have seen or heard:

1. Individual's name: _____________________________

   What that person saw or heard:

2. Individual's name: _____________________________

   What that person saw or heard:

3. Individual's name: _____________________________

   What that person saw or heard:

4. Individual's name: ______________________________

   What that person saw or heard:

(Use additional paper for other people)

Are there other people who might know something else that supports your complaint? ___ No ___ Yes

If yes, please identify each person and what information she or he might have:

1. Individual's name: ______________________________

   What that person saw or heard:

2. Individual's name: ______________________________

   What that person saw or heard:

3. Individual's name: ______________________________

   What that person saw or heard:

(Use additional paper for other people)

Do you have any notes, journals, calendars, e-mails or other papers that show what happened? ___ No ___ Yes

If yes, please provide copies with this statement, or describe where the information can be found:

I HEREBY CERTIFY THAT THE ABOVE INFORMATION IS TRUE AND CORRECT. I UNDERSTAND THAT MAKING FALSE CLAIMS AGAINST OTHER EMPLOYEES IS GROUNDS FOR IMMEDIATE DISCHARGE.

Employee Signature: ______________________ Date: _______________

The second document some trainers recommend is the employer-generated memo confirming what the interviewee said during the interview. Generally, these documents demonstrate that you actually did listen to the employee, so long as nothing critical is left out of the memo. If you use this memo, it is imperative that you take good notes during the interview. The memo has the same purpose as the employee-generated statement — to avoid misunderstandings and to pin down the employee's story. Employees should be given a chance to review the memo, and you may even ask that they sign it to indicate they have read it, but that is not necessary. Employees tend to read the memos as they take them seriously and will let you know if anything is left out or if there were things they forgot to tell you. If such a memo is to be used, it is important that it be written shortly after the interview and presented to the employee within a few business days. Otherwise, preparation of the memo may result in a delay in the investigation, making the employee lose confidence in the system.

Not all investigations are so complicated as to require a confirmatory memo. If the problem is relatively straightforward and will only require that one or two witnesses be interviewed in order for a determination to be made, there is not much to be accomplished by giving such a memo to the employee. If, however, the employee has complained about a pattern of behavior over many months, with many different witnesses, involving many policies, putting the "who saw what when" in writing will help you to plan your investigation and ensure nothing is missed.

At a minimum, the memo should: identify the issues raised; identify the facts provided by the employee during the interview to support the employee's view; confirm these are the only facts and issues; identify who will be the investigator, and that the employee believes the investigator is fair and impartial; identify individuals named as witnesses; identify any other items, including documents, identified by the employee as being helpful; and remind the employee of the necessity of confidentiality and continued cooperation. You may also want to include information on how the investigation will be conducted, although that is not really an employee's concern. And, if the employee takes the memo literally, if you deviate at all from that information, the employee may start to suspect something is wrong with the process. If the memo accurately reflects what the employee told you, and the employee agrees with it, you have an excellent starting point for planning your investigation. An example memo follows:

MEMORANDUM

TO: Jane Doe

FROM: Ingrid Investigator

DATE: September 1, 2005

RE: Your concerns of August 28, 2005

This memo will confirm the discussion we had in my office on August 28, 2005 in which you raised various concerns you have about your supervisor, John Smith. You believe Mr. Smith is harassing you because of the following:

- he has made comments about your clothing, noting it looks African;
- he has made comments about your facial features that make you uncomfortable and indicate he's focusing on your race;
- other employees have told you he makes comments about how you look;
- he frequently asks you how black people take care of their hair; and
- you have overheard him telling racist jokes and talking about the Klan.

You identified Sally Smug, Polly Pureheart, Nick Nice, and Rick Rabble as individuals who have observed Mr. Smith's actions or to whom he has made statements about you.

You could not provide specific dates as to when these incidents occurred, but did indicate they have been occurring continuously over the past three months. You also indicated you did not have any information to give me that would help in the investigation.

If I have missed anything, or if you have additional information to add, please let me know as soon as you can so these allegations can be investigated. As indicated during our discussion, I will be the one investigating your concerns and you agreed and believe I will be fair and impartial and that you are comfortable with my conducting the investigation.

It may be necessary for me to discuss these matters with you again during my investigation. The Company expects your continued cooperation so that we may reach an appropriate resolution. It is also imperative that you keep our discussions confidential and that you do not talk about the investigation with anyone in the company other than me. Information I collect during the investigation will be shared only with those employees who have a need to know. The Company respects employees' rights to bring legitimate concerns and problems to the Company's attention, and the Company prohibits retaliation against such individuals. In the event you feel any information is not being kept confidential and limited to those who have a need to know, or that you are being retaliated against by anyone, please let me know immediately.

Please let me know if this memo does not accurately reflect our discussion or if you have any additional questions or concerns.

Ingrid Investigator

CHAPTER 5

PLANNING THE INVESTIGATION

A. Is it confidential?

Once you have decided that an investigation is warranted, you should plan on what you will do and the order in which you will do it. It is important to remember that almost everything you do, collect, or say during an investigation will be revealed at some point if there is any challenge to the actions taken as a result of the investigation or a challenge to the conduct of the investigation itself. If you believe there is information that will be revealed during the investigation that must remain confidential, contact your legal counsel for advice. While there are ways to protect information, such as proprietary or trade secret information, if you do not carefully dot all the i's and cross all the t's, you will probably lose your right to retain that confidentiality.

B. Who should investigate?

Before you take the next step, you should ask yourself if you are the appropriate investigator. Even if the employee believes you can investigate it, for various reasons you may not be the appropriate individual. For example, if you had a relationship before you worked for the company with the employee about whom the complaint was made, it may be inappropriate for you to investigate. Or, if you advised the manager or were involved in the underlying action, it may be better to assign someone else to be the investigator. It may be that there are very technical financial issues involved that are outside your scope of experience. In that case, it might be better to have an investigator who understands and can interpret company financial data. Or, because of the complainant involved, you may find it hard to be objective, especially if you have handled a lot of the employee's complaints in the past and already doubt her credibility. There can be many reasons you are not appropriate to conduct the investigation and it is up to you to honestly identify them. Remember, your goals are to resolve a dispute and avoid litigation, not create more issues that need to be resolved.

C. Setting up the file

Whoever goes forward with the investigation should set up an investigation file. Information obtained from employees should be maintained in this file, not in the individual employees' personnel files. The file should be kept in a place not readily accessible to employees so that no one can compromise the investigation by reading the file. Your notes should remain confidential throughout the investigation. Do not allow others to review, and worse yet, revise your notes during the investigation as that may convince an employee or a jury that the investigation was not fair and impartial, but was rigged by a member of management.

If your investigation will involve review of medical information, such as in investigations involving the Americans with Disabilities Act ("ADA") or the Family and Medical Leave Act ("FMLA") obligations, be sure you make arrangements for that information to be kept in a separate confidential investigations file. Both the ADA and FMLA have statutory requirements regarding disclosure of medical information and they apply to employment investigations. If you have any doubt about what information you may ask for or review and how to handle that information, consult your legal counsel at the beginning of your investigation.

D. Determining how the investigation should be conducted

What you are investigating will determine how you should investigate it. All investigations will be handled a little bit differently than others, depending upon the issues raised, the obligations that are triggered and the nature of the complaint. The key to determining how to proceed will be to ensure you understand what the real issues are. If you have effectively interviewed the complaining employee, you will have already identified those issues. The next step is to identify whether the issue involves legal obligations or other obligations under company policies and procedures.

If a complainant contends that he or she is being treated differently on account of his or her membership in a protected class, you should be cognizant of your obligations under local, state, and federal discrimination statutes. If those statutes apply, you may have to gather information on similarly situated individuals to determine if the complainant has been treated differently than other employees. If the complaint involves application of company policy, you may need to determine how the policy is applied, if it is applied consistently, and if not applied consistently, the reasons for any discrepancies. You will also need to know if there is room for any discretion under the applicable policy and how that discretion is applied. Once you have a handle on these obligations, it will be easier to identify what additional information you will need to gather during the investigation in order to help you reach a reasonable conclusion. It will also help you identify any additional assistance you will require during the investigation.

E. Gathering and reviewing documents

The first step is to identify any company policies and procedures that may apply to the complaint and review them. If the employee has complained that company business is being conducted at strip clubs at company expense, you might want to review your expense reimbursement policy. If the employee alleges another employee is overriding the hours employees are working, you probably need to review you timecard or clocking in policy. If an employee is complaining about not being given a new position because of a bad performance review, you will probably want to review the performance appraisal policy as well as any promotion or transfer policies. Your knowledge of the company and the complaint will help you to identify the policies and procedures you need to review. Any policies or procedures that are reviewed should be copied and made a part of your investigation file.

The next step will be to identify any other documents that should be reviewed that are specific to the complaint, such as expense reports and performance reviews. In almost every case you will want to review the personnel files of the complainant and target of the investigation, and possibly of the witnesses, as well. While you need not include copies of the entire files in your investigation file, you will want to make copies of documents that you believe will be relevant to the investigation or which contain additional information that is helpful.

Occasionally, if there is time between receiving the complaint and the initial meeting with the employee, an investigator will review the personnel files of the complainant and the target. On one hand, reviewing the files may give the investigator a better idea of the relationship between the parties and allow the investigator to develop and ask better questions. On the other hand, the investigator may not want to risk developing any preconceived notions about either party and will wait until the determination of whether an investigation is required is made. Neither way is more correct than the other. How it is done is a matter of personal style. Since the goal is to be able to demonstrate a thorough and effective investigation was conducted resulting in a good faith determination of what occurred, the order in which the files were reviewed should not be relevant so long as the investigator remained objective.

If the complaint is one concerning discriminatory discipline, you may also need to review the files of other employees who were disciplined in similar situations. These individuals usually will not be identified by the complainant or the target, but must be discovered by talking to the department manager, other supervisors, or the appropriate employees in the human resources department.

Companies document and retain more information than at any time in the past. Storage of such information has become easier with technology. Therefore, if you want information, chances are you can find it within your organization. When it comes to documents, sometimes the more you ask for, the more you get.

F. Identifying who will be interviewed

After identifying the documents to be gathered and reviewed, the next step is to identify the individuals to be interviewed. Of course, the target will be interviewed, as will any individuals identified by the complainants as witnesses or observers. That may not be all you should interview, however. You should consider interviewing the authors of any documents, such as performance appraisals or shopping reports. There may be other people who have information you think is relevant that were not identified by the complainant. For example, you may want to talk to the department manager to see how certain policies have historically been applied in the department. You are not limited to interviewing only those persons identified by the complainant.

You should also plan on expanding your list of interviewees after you talk to the target of the investigation and that individual may give you names of others who were present or who will contradict the complainant's story. If the target gives you names of individuals to interview and you fail to contact them, you risk a finding that you did not conduct a complete investigation and that your findings were not based upon good faith. Therefore, when planning on when to conduct the interviews and trying to determine how long it will take to complete your investigation, consider that you will identify more tasks as the investigation proceeds. It is because of these unknown factors that you cannot always tell an employee by when the investigation will be complete.

G. Setting the order of the interviews

If you watch a lot of police or crime shows on television, you know that the "perp" is usually the last one interviewed. The police try to gather as many facts as they can before confronting the perp. One of the reasons is because they cannot control who people talk to or what they say after they have been interviewed. Employers, however, do have additional control that can be exercised and enforced through disciplinary action. Therefore, it is best to make your perp, or the target of the investigation, the next one you interview after the complainant. Why? You want to pin down what the target has to say and find out exactly what facts are in dispute. A police investigation starts with the knowledge that a crime has been committed and is designed to determine who committed the crime. An employment investigation is designed to resolve factual issues to determine if there is any problem. The best way to crystallize what the disputes are is to get the target's side of the story. There will be facts that are not in dispute, and you will be able to identify these best by talking to the target. If there are matters not in dispute, you do not want to spend time with other witnesses trying to determine what happened.

In Chapter 11, you will learn more about defamation claims that may be asserted as the result of statements made during an investigation. One way to possibly avoid such claims is to talk to the target of the investigation first. Defamation claims arise when false statements about an individual are repeated to those who do not have a need to know. If you talk to the target first, you may be able to determine whether some facts are true or not and may not need to investigate them further.

Another reason for interviewing the target first is that it may help to judge the credibility of other witnesses. For example, if the target admits to making a racial joke at a staff meeting, but his supporters all deny that he ever tells any jokes, that will help you evaluate the credibility of the other witnesses. In addition, the target may provide additional information about witnesses identify by the complainant that will help you in your other interviews.

You may be tempted to talk to witnesses identified by the claimant first, in order to get some background information and determine what is actually going on in the area where the complainant works. Although these are good reasons for wanting to talk to others first, you can still get that information from them at a later time. These reasons are not as good as the ones supporting talking to the target before talking to any witnesses.

Assuming you decide to interview the target first, you then need to decide the order in which other witnesses will be interviewed. The first factors to consider will be work related and according to your company's operational needs — the shifts employees work, whether any of them are on vacation, or whether any working on a critical project from which they should not be removed until completed. The next factor will be to determine whether you can preserve the confidentiality of the investigation by talking to employees in a certain order. Although you may have employees sign acknowledgements that they will not discuss the investigation, you know you have employees working for you who simply cannot refrain from gossiping, despite the threat of disciplinary action. If one of those types of employees is one that you will need to interview, you should consider making that employee your last interview so that he does not pollute the investigation in any manner. You may also want to schedule those interviews at the end of the day so after the interview concludes, there is no one for the employee to talk to before returning the next day.

While you want to interview all the individuals identified by the complainant and target, you should only interview individuals necessary to help you gather facts. If the complainant identifies a witness who can say she heard the racial joke, but cannot offer any assistance, it may not be necessary to interview that individual once the target admits to telling the joke. By limiting the number of interviewees, you can stay on track, stay focused on the real issues, and you will use your time more efficiently in arriving at a determination.

Once you have determined the order in which you plan to conduct the interviews, you should schedule them as quickly as possible. First and foremost, particularly where the complaint involves actions occurring over a long period of time, you want to interview the employees before their memories fade. In addition, you do not want to risk employees leaving your company or otherwise becoming unavailable. There is nothing more frustrating to a human resources representative or company lawyer than having to deal with a critical witness who was terminated before the interview was conducted. If that happens, and the employee is no longer friendly to the company, it makes it much harder to judge credibility and determine what happened.

You should also conduct the interviews relatively quickly rather than waiting days between interviews. The more time that passes, the more you risk that employees will hear about the investigation and become tainted by hearing from or talking to other witnesses or just by hearing things through the company grapevine. The less chance there is for gossip to take root, the better chance you have of getting truthful statements from your interviewees.

Before beginning the first interview, you need to decide whether you will have interviewees complete forms acknowledging the confidentiality of the investigation. If you will use those forms, you should have them prepared and available before each interview starts.

Determining where to conduct the interviews is also critical. Each interview should be conducted separately and in a location where other employees will not overhear you. There is no need to conduct the interviews in a secret location or off-site. You just need to ensure you have a secure area where you can talk in private.

H. Is expert help needed?

If the need for expert assistance was not apparent when you considered the nature of the complaint and the type of investigation to conduct, your next step will be to determine if you will need assistance from any experts, either within or outside your company. Assume that the complaint is that an employee is using the computer to override employees' time entries, resulting in overtime not being paid. In such a case, you should contact your IT people to see if logs exist showing when such overrides were made, under whose ID, and from which computers. If only supervisors can override time, but the IT people can demonstrate the target logged in on her computer, entered her time, and logged out, then within ten seconds the supervisor's password was used to log in at the same computer to make a few overrides, then signed out, it may indicate the target is indeed making changes. Knowing the sequence of how things occurred may help you interview the target, either in the initial interview or a follow-up interview.

Another area in which expertise is commonly needed is to identify or retrieve e-mails that were sent or received from certain accounts or computers. Unfortunately, this information may take a while to gather, so you may have to conduct your investigation while the IT people work on collecting the e-mails. The order in which you talk to experts is not critical, but it may help streamline the process if you have information from them before conducting witness interviews.

Be creative when thinking about where you might be able to find assistance. For example, if an employee's complaint is about not receiving a reasonable accommodation for a disability, you might want to talk to a vocational rehabilitation expert, not just the department manager. This will not only help your investigation, it could further insulate your company from liability in an ADA action as compensatory and punitive damages are not available when the employer makes a good faith effort to provide an accommodation, even if the employer's actions are eventually determined to have been incorrect.

I. Drafting your questions

Proper preparation is essential to conducting an effective interview. Before your first interview, you should draft the questions you plan to ask each interviewee. If you do not plan these questions in advance, you risk forgetting to ask about something critical or being led off track by a recalcitrant witness. Different people have different ways of writing up questions — some use handwritten notes, others type out the exact questions, leaving room for notes after each question. You should use whatever style you are most comfortable with and that allows you to focus on and record the important facts that come out of each interview. And you should be flexible enough to ask additional questions depending upon what you learn in an interview. Once an interview is completed, you should review your draft questions for other employees to see what additional information you should ask about or how your draft should be revised to help you gather all the necessary facts.

The best way to start drafting your questions is to outline the issues about which you need information. The answers to the initial questions will invariably lead to additional questions and having an outline helps you stay on track. It is usually helpful to ask questions in chronological order as well as a logical basis will help you unravel what actually happened. You need to understand what facts you will need to have in order to make a determination in order to know what questions to ask and you need to find a logical way of making sure you ask the right questions to gather these facts.

Similar to the questions you asked in the initial interview, your questions should be broad and open-ended, not questions that only require a "yes" or "no" answer. Once the interviewee starts answering your questions, you can ask follow-up questions seeking to narrow down the precise facts the interviewee knows. Again, you should also avoid legalese. Use clear, simple language and ask simple, understandable questions. Avoid asking compound questions or questions that assume a fact to be true. For example, if you ask, "Did you see or did you know Jane had problems with John?" and the interviewee answers, "Yes," you do not know if he actually observed an interaction or just heard about it through the grapevine. If you do ask a compound question, follow-up to determine to which part of the question the interviewee was responding.

Focus on the five W's—what, who, when, where, and why. For each incident the interviewee says he witnessed, ask each of these questions to get a precise understanding of what this witness saw happen, when, and where. The more information you can get from an individual, the easier it will be to compare stories when witnesses contradict each other. This comparison may become critical when you are making credibility determinations.

As you will see in Chapter 6, one of your first tasks will be to establish a rapport with the interviewee. Asking tough or confrontational questions at the beginning of the interview is not a good way to accomplish this task. You should not avoid hard questions; you just should not start out the interview with them.

Once you have outlined your questions, you should outline some general comments that you will use to begin each interview, including a general description of what you are investigating, what role the interviewee plays in the investigation, and how you will use the information you learn from the interviewee. In the next chapter, you will learn how to respond to questions that may arise at the beginning of the investigation.

Having completed your outlines of your questions for the interviewees, compare each outline to your notes of your first meeting with the employee to see if there is anything that has been left out. If not, you are ready to begin.

INVESTIGATION PLANNING CHECKLIST

This checklist will help you make sure you properly plan your investigation once you have interviewed the complainant.

- ❑ Identify any obligations that arise from the issues and how the investigation should be conducted.
- ❑ Identify and gather policies and procedures that may apply.
- ❑ Identify other documents, like personnel files or performance appraisals, that you should reviewed, including information on similarly situated employees.
- ❑ Identify the individuals to be interviewed.
- ❑ Determine the order of interviews.
- ❑ Determine if you need expert assistance and talk to those experts.
- ❑ Prepare any confidentiality memos employees will need to sign.
- ❑ Draft all interview questions.
- ❑ Find a private location to conduct the interviews.
- ❑ Set a date and time for all interviews.
- ❑ Allow for review of additional policies, procedures or documents based upon what is learned in the interviews, and review them.
- ❑ Allow for additional interviews, either to follow up or with other individuals identified during the investigation.

CHAPTER 6

CONDUCTING THE INTERVIEWS

Remember, the purpose of the investigation at this point is to gather facts. The better you are at gathering the facts, the better chance you have of conducting an effective investigation and reaching a reasonable result. In planning your investigation, you should have gathered any helpful documentation. You probably would have reviewed at least some of it when drafting your questions. If you haven't reviewed all the documents you have gathered, do so before you interview the target and make any changes to your questions based upon what you learn from the documents.

Interviewing witnesses is one of the most critical aspects of conducting an investigation because it requires you to extract information in such a manner that you can later evaluate and analyze it. Plaintiff's lawyers frequently comment that they do not believe many people can conduct effective investigations due to preconceived notions about their employees. Many plaintiff's lawyers believe that most investigators begin investigations believing the claims to be frivolous and that they will only maintain a facade of objectivity until they get tired of the complainant. It is at that point that something happens to the complainant that plaintiff's lawyers usually find actionable. And, in filing a lawsuit, they make the conduct of the investigation the lynchpin to demonstrate the company had no intention of complying with its legal obligations; it was just going through the paces to try and pacify a troublemaker.

With those thoughts in mind, you can see how important it is that you maintain a calm demeanor and do not do anything to compromise your objectivity. If something comes up during the investigation that you believe taints you as the investigator, you should get someone else involved to complete the investigation. Remember, you want to resolve disputes and avoid litigation, not have your personal motivations put on trial.

Normally, you will not know what type of reaction you will get from the target once you begin the interview and she learns what the purpose is of your meeting. You should anticipate all types of reactions — from anger to noncooperation to total denial to complete cooperation to complete admission (which rarely happens). You should anticipate questions that might arise in any of these situations and be prepared with logical consistent answers, regardless of the demeanor of the target. Although the interview with the target may be the most difficult, other witnesses will present their own unique challenges, and you must be equally as prepared to answer their questions.

Before beginning your interviews, remember the first golden rule—treat others how you would like to be treated. Being interviewed in connection with something that may result in disciplinary action, whether of the interviewee or a colleague, is always somewhat stressful. Witnesses may not want to get someone else in trouble or may not want to get involved. Targets may be fearful that they are about to lose their jobs. In each situation, the interviewee will usually be at least a little apprehensive. Think of how you would feel if you were the one being asked the questions and think how you would like to be treated in such a situation. If you remember what it would be like if the shoe were on the other foot, you would be a more effective interviewer.

As with your initial interview with the complainant, you want to put the interviewee at ease. It is not necessary, however, to ensure that the interviewee is comfortable with the fact that you are the interviewer. If investigators asked that question of everyone you interviewed, no one would ever be qualified as there would probably always be at least one objection, particularly if the interviewee believed the investigation could be brought to a halt with a complaint about the investigator.

In many cases, the interviewee will not know why he or she is being interviewed. The opening comments you prepared when you drafted your questions should help you put the individual at ease.

Your comments, however, will differ slightly for the target from what you will say to other witnesses.

A. Special considerations for interviewing the target

You will have to identify what is being investigated to the target or you will never be able to determine what matters are in dispute or gather facts. At the beginning of the investigation, you need not identify who made the complaint as long as you identify the issue being investigated. For example, if an employee reported to you that his boss is being reimbursed twice for expenses, once off hotel receipts and once off his charge card bills, you can just tell the target that you are investigating the falsification of expense reports. It is not necessary for him to know how you found out. If you just ask broad-based questions of the target without providing at least some background information, it will take forever for you to gather relevant facts. Remember, you want to do an efficient, as well as effective, investigation and you do not want to waste hours of time.

Once you identify what you are investigating, you should explain to the target that the purpose of this meeting is to allow you to gather facts and identify issues. In many cases, the target will try to ask questions or make demands. You should explain that you need to ask the questions and that cooperation will be helpful. Do not let the target take control of the interview by asking questions.

You should also explain to the target that you want as much information from him that he can provide to help you make an appropriate determination. Explain that his input is important and that you want him to provide any and all information that he thinks will be helpful in determining what occurred.

Occasionally, a target will refuse to cooperate. Some employers try to threaten employees into talking, informing them that if they do not participate, they will be terminated. Those practices, however, have not been found to be effective in gathering facts or in getting targets to be truthful or cooperative. If a target refuses to cooperate, you should explain that you have an obligation to complete the investigation and are prepared to do so without his participation if that is his choice. You can also tell him that his refusal to cooperate will be taken into consideration when making the final determination. Finally, reinforce how important you think any facts he has will be in making your decision. Most targets, when they realize the investigation will continue with or without them, tend to be willing to talk at this point.

Another tactic of targets is to demand that the individual making the allegations join you in the interview. Some targets will even claim they have a constitutional right to be confronted by their accusers. Such a right exists when the government is involved, as in criminal proceedings, but it has no application in the private sector, such as employment matters. Therefore, no right to confrontation exists. When confronted with such a demand, you should tell the target that it is not necessary and that you just want to gather the facts and hear his side of the story.

If you did bring in the complainant, you could fatally damage you internal complaint and investigation process as employees will not complain if they are afraid of being put in the hot seat and being subject to a nasty confrontation. If the target insists, ask the target what questions he would ask the complainant and make notes of them. Do not promise to ask all the questions. Just inform the target that you will get back to him if necessary.

If the target does indicate anger at the complainant or is in a management position, you should be particularly careful to stress the company policy against retaliation and warn the target that if he retaliates against anyone in any manner as a result of this complaint or investigation, he will be subject to disciplinary action, possibly even termination of employment.

At the end of the interview, you can tell the target who the complainant is and specifically what he has been accused of by the complainant. That will give the target one more chance to provide information to you. If the target just denies everything, go back to your "why" questions. See if the target has any reason that would explain why the complainant made untrue allegations. By asking why, you can explore the possible motivation of the complainant and you may learn more facts that will help in the investigation.

B. General interview guidelines

Except as set forth in section A, these guidelines are equally applicable to interviews with targets. Each interviewee should be told, in very general terms, what you are investigating, what role the interviewee plays in the investigation, how you will use the information you learn from the interviewee. It is not uncommon for an interviewee to ask, "Can I get in any trouble?" You should never answer "no" as the interviewee may view that as a grant of immunity and tell you all kinds of things that she has done for which she now thinks she has a free pass. Instead, you should emphasize that the interviewee is not the target of the investigation, and you are just gathering facts. If it turns out that the interviewee is an accomplice, there probably will be negative implications.

An interviewee may also ask who else is being interviewed as part of the investigation. Identification of those individuals should not matter one way or another to the interviewee. You can tell the interviewee that you are not revealing the identity of whom you are talking to, just as you will not tell others that she has been interviewed.

Some interviewees may be hesitant to participate in the interview because they believe a decision has already been reached and that they have nothing to gain by talking to you. You should do what you can to convince the employee that the purpose of the investigation is to gather information so that a decision can be reached and that none has been reached as of this time. You can also inform the employee that you take the obligation to investigate employee complaints very seriously and that when employees raise issues, you must investigate them. It is only at the end of thorough investigations that any decisions can be made.

It is important that, at the beginning of the interview, interviewees understand the importance of maintaining the confidentiality of the investigation. You should stress that no one involved in the investigation is to discuss the matter with anyone other than you and that anyone who does discuss the investigation will be disciplined as appropriate. You may also want to let the interviewee know that if she attempts to interfere with anyone else's interview, or with the investigation in any manner, that action will also lead to disciplinary action. If you require interviewees to sign written acknowledgements, you should present it to them at this time, give them sufficient time to read it, then have them sign it and return it to you. It may also be appropriate to inform the employee that the company does not tolerate retaliation or negative actions being taken against them because they participated in the investigation and if they feel that happens, they should report it to you immediately.

In some instances, when the interviewee realizes someone else is being investigated and might get disciplined, the interviewee may indicate she will participate so long as you inform her of the results of the investigation. You should explain that, like all personnel decisions, they are not shared with other employees. For example, if the interviewee were disciplined, the interviewee would not want that information shared with other employees in the workplace.

At this point in the interview, it should be clear the interviewee is going to cooperate, at least to some extent. The interviewee should then be informed what you expect from her. Now is a good time to stress the seriousness of the investigation and that you are seeking to collect facts to determine what happened. You should also state that it is very important that you obtain truthful and accurate facts. You are not looking for opinions, but facts — what the interviewee saw or knows firsthand. You also do not want the interviewee to speculate as to what might or might not have happened. It is what the interviewee knows that is most important. If the interviewee balks, or refuses to cooperate, you should inform the interviewee that failure to cooperate could result in disciplinary action. This should be handled differently than a target refusing to cooperate because a target may be fearful of self-incrimination and is the one most likely to suffer the consequences of any adverse determinations. The interviewee, on the other hand, may have information the company requires in order to satisfy its obligations and the interviewee must understand the consequences of failing to provide that information when requested.

Once you get into fact gathering, follow the outline you have prepared so that you can cover all the issues and try to get information in a chronological fashion. Although you will deviate from that outline based upon answers to other questions, your outline should serve as the basis to keep you on track.

Although it seems elementary, do not ask more than one question at a time. Some interviewers get uncomfortable when a witness does not answer a question and rather than endure the silence, they ask another question. When you start asking more questions, you cannot be sure what the individual is answering or you risk intimidating the witness further by piling on the questions. And, most importantly, if you are doing most of the talking, you are not being effective and not accomplishing your goal of resolving a dispute.

C. Ending the interview

Just as you should develop opening comments to be used for all interviews, you also have some closing remarks to make when the interview is over. Once you have asked all the questions you have, you should ask the interviewee if there are any other individuals she knows of who may be able to provide you with additional facts that could be helpful in the investigation. If not, you should review critical facts the interviewee told you to make sure there is no dispute over what the interviewee said. This will also give you a chance to ask the interviewee if there is anything else she wants to tell you.

Reemphasizing the confidential nature of the investigation and asking the interviewee to come to you with any questions, comments, or, if she thinks of other facts, witnesses, or documents that could help you, will help maintain the integrity of your investigation. Depending upon who the target is, you may also want to remind the interviewee of the policy against retaliation. Finally, ask the interviewee if she has any questions.

One common question is "what happens now?" You should not provide specific information about how you plan to conduct the investigation, but only indicate that you will be collecting additional facts to help you reach a determination. A question targets often ask is "when will you be done with the investigation?" While you might have every intention of completing your interviews within the next day, you should never promise a target that you will have a decision by a specific date and time. Employee schedules change, you may find it necessary to interview more individuals, and you may have to clear your recommendation with several levels of management, before it can be implemented. Therefore, you should indicate that you are conducting the investigation as quickly as you can and provide just a general estimate of when you hope the investigation will be completed, such as within the next two weeks. That way, you do not raise false expectations. Once the interviewee has asked all questions, thank her for her cooperation. After she leaves, it is time to review your notes and make any additional ones.

D. Dealing with difficult witnesses

Unfortunately, witnesses do not present all the information you need in a logical, rational fashion. Nor do they just give you relevant information. Some witnesses will weave their life story into the interview, analogizing to things that happened to them. Some of these witnesses may make you want to pull your hair out, but your job is to figure out how to deal with them. While some witnesses may be inarticulate, it just takes patience usually to find out what they know. While frustrating, those interviewees do not generally require any "special handling." There are, however, different types of witnesses who do require that you recognize their styles and know how to interview them. The type of witness you are interviewing will not change the basic questions you have prepared, but it probably will change the way in which the witness is approached and require that you ask additional questions in order to learn anything from them.

1. In complete denial

Every once in a while, either a target or a witness will deny everything. Not just one or two things — they issue a blanket denial. They did not do it, did not see it, or were not involved. Sort of like the Sergeant Schultz character from the *Hogan's Heroes* television series who always said, "I know nothink!" Blanket denials, however, do nothing toward helping you determine what happened. The first question that arises when you run into such an individual is how to get him to talk. One of the best ways is to ask "why" and try to uncover what the interviewee believes the motivation might be for someone to say something occurred if the witness absolutely denies it occurred. Although you may initially get an "I don't know" response, most people eventually cannot resist offering at least an opinion about others. If you can get any type of response, it might provide the opening for you to ask more probing questions.

You should also try to determine if there are other issues the interviewee is trying to hide by making these denials. For example, is the individual on the final step of the progressive discipline program and ready to be terminated? If so, maybe the individual is fearful that talking about his boss can do no good and will only ensure his termination. It will take creativity to get the interviewee to talk about the job and what may be going on, but if you can uncover other issues, you may find the reason for the denials.

If an interviewee persists in denying everything, assess his or her credibility by asking questions about things that others have told you about the interviewee's involvement with the situation. If he continues to deny things that you already know occurred, that would tend to indicate his denials are full of holes.

It is important that you distinguish between denials and failure to remember. A witness may tell you he simply does not recall. This answer is the best for a witness trying to be evasive and the worst for an investigator trying to uncover facts. A witness can change his story later by saying he remembered what happened after talking to other witnesses or reviewing documents. The investigator may look foolish for not finding ways to refresh the witness' memory during the investigation. Therefore, if a witness switches from a flat denial to not recalling anything, keep asking questions to find out what the witness does recall. Again, you will have to be creative with your questions to find a way to get the witness to talk.

2. Uncooperative

An interviewee may not deny everything, but may be uncooperative nonetheless. Such witnesses tend to be defensive. They may believe something is going to happen to them or they may be trying to protect a friend or boss who is the target of the investigation. As with a witness who denies everything, you will need to be patient and continue to ask questions. Most witnesses cannot resist the temptation to start talking if the questioning continues.

One of the first ways to get an uncooperative witness to start talking is to explore why the witness does not want to cooperate. Once the witness starts answering questions, it will usually be easier to get the witness to start answering the questions you really want answered. Interviews with uncooperative witnesses may take longer and you will need patience. If you are not patient, however, you risk missing important facts in your investigation.

3. Center of attention

These witnesses love being the center of attention — it makes them feel important and needed. You should not ignore these witnesses, but you must be careful to focus on the facts and credibility issues, so you can make a reasonable determination of what is true and what is exaggerated to make the witness look more important or what is really just the witness' opinion. If an individual focuses too much on how something or someone affects her, instead of focusing on the facts, you need to ask questions designed to get the witness focusing on something other than herself. Again, creativity is the clue.

4. Has that ax to grind

These witnesses will use the interview to complain about other employees, retaliate against who they believe the target of the investigation to be, or complain about policies and procedures they think need to be changed. There is something bothering the witness that can be wholly unrelated to the investigation at hand and the witness sees the interview as the chance to get everything out in the open. Like those who like the limelight, you should not ignore these witnesses, but you should temper what you learn from them and try to get them focusing on the issues in the investigation.

You should also be aware that during these types of interviews you might learn of other problems that need to be investigated. If that is the case, you should inform the witness that you think the issue he or she has raised is very important and should not get confused with the current investigation. Depending upon the nature of the complaint, you may want to separate the interview session into two parts; the first part designed to assist you with the investigation at hand, and the second part designed to be your initial interview in a potentially new investigation. Or, if you believe it is appropriate, tell the witness that you would like to schedule another interview to talk about the additional problems when you have more time, because it is important to you. Before the interview concludes, set a time to talk to the witness about the new issues. In either case, do not let your focus on the instant investigation blind you to other problems that you might uncover.

E. Taking notes

As set forth in Chapter 4.B, taking notes instead of tape recording interviews normally results in a more candid interview. But you must learn how to take effective notes in order for them to be helpful to you and to demonstrate that you conducted an effective investigation. Notes taken during an investigation need not be grammatically perfect or be in your best handwriting. Nor must you always use complete sentences. It is more important to focus on the information you are receiving instead of the form of your notes.

You should never plan to throw out or rewrite your notes. If you do that, a plaintiff's attorney will argue that the original notes contained the "real facts" but you rewrote your notes to reflect only what you thought would be in the company's best interest. If your handwriting is such that no one else can read it easily, you can type your notes, but you should type exactly what is written in your notes and maintain your handwritten notes as well. Investigators who add a lot of extraneous information to the notes, intending to rewrite them before the investigation is completed, will invariably write something inappropriate and forget to rewrite those notes. But you should not hesitate to add facts to your notes after the interview is completed to make sure you do not leave out anything important. When gathering facts from the witness, it may be difficult to also write down your factual observations concerning demeanor. In those cases, you definitely want to make sure you supplement your notes after finishing the interview, as factual observations may be critical in helping you resolve credibility issues.

If you have a hesitant witness whom you are having trouble engaging, it may be necessary to abandon your note taking to concentrate on the witness. Do not worry—you will remember the important things and you can write them down immediately after the interview ends. Some people are uncomfortable answering questions for someone writing everything down, but they are much more willing to talk when the pen is put down. Others think if their comments are written down, they will get in trouble, no matter what assurances you give them. You need to recognize when note taking is interfering with fact gathering and act appropriately. Your need to write down what you learn should never interfere with the rapport you need to develop with the witness or indicate you are not really interested in what he or she has to say.

What should be in your notes? Your notes should only include facts and factual observations. It is not critical to get everything down word for word as long as you get the facts. Remember the investigation was triggered by some factual dispute, and it is your job to gather as many facts as you can to resolve that dispute. If you only write down your conclusions and opinions, instead of the facts, it will be difficult to assess a witness' credibility, and you will leave out critical information you may need later to resolve disputes between witnesses or even to recognize discrepancies between witness statements. Compare the following two statements:

> The interview with Nancy began at 3:10. Denied knowing anything at all. I think she's lying. She's hiding something by denying it all.

> Nancy showed up ten minutes late for her interview at 3:10 p.m. She was twisting a rubber band and not making eye contact the whole time. I asked her if she ever saw Murray and Alice together. She said no. Asked if ever saw Murray and Alice together near the copy machine. Hesitated for a couple minutes, looked down, said she never did. She asked if she could go. I asked why. She had a lot to do for Murray and didn't want him to know she was gone.

The first statement does not offer any assistance in resolving facts or assessing credibility. It contains only the investigator's conclusions regarding Nancy. If a lawsuit is filed and several years later the investigator is asked what supported those conclusions, there is a good chance the investigator will not remember. The second statement, on the other hand, provides information from which the investigator can later remember why Nancy was nervous and what her apparent concern was. Your notes should be similar to that example.

After the interview is over, but before you begin another, you should supplement your notes with your factual observations. Those include the witness' demeanor and whether the answers were logical and consistent. You may also want to make some notes as to whether you have learned anything from other witnesses or documents that substantiates what you learned in the latest interview. Finally, if you think other facts exist that tend to demonstrate something this witness said that was true or not true, you can jot down those facts as well. All of these additional notes will help you in determining whom to believe in the event there are still disputes after you speak to everyone.

Throughout the investigation you should keep your notes confidential and not share them with anyone, particularly not with the target or other witnesses. There is nothing to be gained by letting others review your notes, as they will start asking questions and try to take control of the interview of the investigation. That can only make your fact-finding job more difficult. And remember, the purpose of the notes is to document your findings and to help you make a final determination, not to serve as a basis for debate with witnesses.

F. Assessing credibility

There is an old line that if three people are eyewitnesses to the same car accident, you will get four different versions of what occurred. This can occur because different people perceive things in different ways. It can also occur because of the different viewpoints from which the accident is seen. Or, the passage of time may cause people to forget details that seemed minor to them at the time of the accident. The result is that you may have three people telling the truth, as they believe it.

You may also have a situation where one or more witnesses are not being truthful. Maybe one of the eyewitnesses had a crush on the young girl who caused the accident, so he "forgets" that he never saw her brake lights come on. Or maybe one witness thinks the injured person is a crybaby who is not entitled to get a lot of money for a small wreck. Of course, most witnesses will never admit these biases and you may never discover them. What you will be required to do when you have different stories is to determine who is more credible; that is, who is more believable, and why. Remember, what you need to do at the end of the investigation is to be able to articulate a reasonable basis to support your conclusions.

There are different things you should consider in assessing a person's credibility. The first is the individual's demeanor during the interview. Body language is a good indicator of demeanor. If an individual refuses to look you in the eye and stays very nervous, you should wonder why, and if that tends to provide a reason not to trust them. Be careful, however, that you are aware of any cultural difference that may account for such body language. For example, if this is a female employee's first job, and she is from a culture where you do not look superiors in the eye when addressing them, you should not consider the fact that eye contact was not made to be an indicator of truth or falsity.

It is also important to note if an individual's demeanor changes during an interview. In most cases, when you bring up more serious questions, there will be some change in a person's demeanor. But, if there is a drastic change, it may indicate the individual is no longer being truthful or is hiding something. For example, assume you are asking an employee whether she has ever had problems with people she supervised and she says not that she recalls. You then present to her comments from an employee on a performance review she prepared that said she was rude and abusive. If the employee immediately gets defensive, but continues to deny she ever knew about any complaint, that demeanor change should also change how you view her credibility.

You should also consider how the individual reacted to your questions and whether he inspired confidence in you—did you find the individual to be believable. In addition, you should consider whether the individual freely answered your questions or whether you had to struggle to get any information from the individual. All these behaviors in answering questions will be things that impact how credible you find someone to be.

Logic and common sense will also play a part in determining how credible a person is. A witness may be very confident and comfortable with answering your questions, but may relate a situation that could not have logically occurred. If an employee tells you she could not have taken a piece of equipment because she was working in another part of the building that day, but the employee is the only one who had a key to the locked room where the equipment was located, there is a logical inconsistency that would seem to indicate the individual is not being truthful.

You should also consider how witnesses' stories relate to one another. If three witnesses relate the same chronology of events, yet the fourth witness tells a completely different story, the lack of consistency should alert you to consider whether the individual is credible. If the inconsistency becomes apparent during the interview, you can ask the individual to try to explain any discrepancies that may exist to see if the witness has a plausible explanation. There may be a perfectly plausible explanation and the other three witnesses may have decided to tell the same story, but unless you ask questions designed to find out "why" you might not have the information you need to determine who is credible.

Corroborating evidence can also be used to determine who is telling the truth. In the O.J. Simpson trial, many thought Mark Furman was the perfect witness—calm, confident, forthcoming—until he denied ever using a racial slur. The testimony of others who could relate specific instances, citing times and dates, of his use of such slurs totally destroyed his credibility. If you have doubts about a witness, see if there are other types of evidence that tend to prove or disprove that witness' version.

With today's technology, finding such corroborating evidence may be easier than you realize. Suppose an employee is being disciplined for not following up and keeping her boss informed on a regular basis. The employee thinks she is being discriminated against because of her race, but her boss says he never hears from her when she is traveling and that makes it difficult for him to manage the business. In today's world, it is hard to imagine anyone without a cell phone. If the employee says she talked to her boss everyday, ask her for cell phone or calling card bills. If the bills show calls were made to the boss' number every day and that each call was billed for an average of seven minutes, that evidence tends to corroborate her story, not his. Computer records and e-mails showing when a computer was in use or when an e-mail was sent are similar types of corroborating evidence that may be helpful to you in resolving disputed facts.

Other corroborating evidence may come from admissions made by the witness or by others. If one of the complaints is that the guys pass around Victoria Secret catalogs and several males admit they do that, it tends to indicate they are credible. After all, why would witnesses admit something they think might get them in trouble if it were not true? If all the males interviewed admit it and even tell you in which drawer the catalog is kept, the target's denial of ever having seen a catalog is not worthy of credence.

Even when direct corroborating evidence does not exist, there may be circumstantial evidence. This type of evidence consists of facts from which you can deduce what probably happened. One of the most common ways to get circumstantial evidence when a witness acts in a manner that seems inappropriate is to ask how the witness reacts in similar situations. For example, what if you are confronted with a complaint that a supervisor routinely calls the employee into his office, with no one else present, and yells and screams obscenities at the employee when criticizing performance. If the supervisor totally denies ever having raised his voice, you should ask other employees how he normally reacts to stressful situations. If others tell you he's known for flying off the handle and yelling, that circumstantial evidence may tend to prove his behavior was consistent with the employee who complained and that his total and absolute denial simply is not credible.

Or assume you have a department of recent college graduates, all of whom are male, supervised by a woman at least 15 years older than all of them who is accused of trying to get employees to go out with her. The newest employee complains she invited him out to dinner and offered to have sex after dinner was over, implying it would be good for his career. She admits to taking him to dinner, like she does all employees, but denies anything inappropriate occurred. Upon learning she takes all her employees to dinner, you interview the others, who admit not only that she did the same, but several also admit they had sex with her after dinner. This type of behavior tends to demonstrate it probably occurred with the newest employee as well.

The task of assessing credibility is like putting together a giant puzzle. Knowing what to look for and how to find other types of evidence are clues you can use to help you make the pieces fit together. If you cannot make the pieces fit together or nothing makes sense, you should revisit who you believed and why, and possibly interview the witnesses further. If you can reasonably explain the factors on which you chose to believe one witness over another, you will help demonstrate that you made a good faith determination about what happened.

CHAPTER 7

SUSPENDING EMPLOYEES DURING THE INVESTIGATION

There will be occasions where an employer cannot wait until the end of the investigation and must take action against one or more employees either after meeting with the complainant or before the investigation is complete. Whether interim action is necessary will depend upon the nature of the allegations and the conduct of individuals during the investigation. Most interim actions involve removing someone from the workplace, either the target or the complainant, during the investigation. These immediate actions are usually necessary in order to protect either the employees or company property.

Allegations involving actual or threatened violence or physical assault may require you to remove the target from the workplace in order to conduct an investigation. Or, you may want to send the complainant home while you conduct your investigation. Whether to suspend someone from employment or otherwise remove them from the workplace during an investigation can be the most difficult decision an employer must make during an investigation. Remember, however, that such action is not final and that you will have the opportunity to return the employee to work if the investigation indicates it would be appropriate not to take any adverse action or to issue discipline less severe than termination.

If the allegations involve criminal misconduct, you may also want to remove the target from the workplace in order to prevent further conduct from occurring or in order to prevent the target from possibly destroying critical evidence. In such situations, you should also be concerned about whether any criminal liability may be imputed to the company because of the level of the employee accused of misconduct or because the company may be found to have condoned the activity. Whenever you find out about potential criminal activity, you should consult your lawyer to determine exactly what needs to be done to protect the company.

There may also be allegations of ongoing misconduct that, if occurring, could seriously damage the company if allowed to continue, such as in embezzlement cases. In those cases, until you know what, if anything, is happening, it may be in the company's interest to remove the potential problem from the workplace until the matter is sorted out.

In addition to allegations that require you to consider removing someone from the workplace at the beginning of the investigation, there may be incidents that occur during the investigation that require you to send an employee home. The most common situation where this is required is when the target interferes with the investigation or where it becomes necessary to protect employees from retaliation. It can also occur if a witness continually violates the confidentiality requirements or otherwise interferes with and pollutes your investigation.

There are several matters you must take into consideration in determining whether to suspend the target of the investigation. First, if you have decided suspension is necessary, do you announce your decision to the target before or after your interview with the target? You should assume that informing the target of your decision will not be a pleasant experience and it may hinder your ability to obtain necessary information. Remember, you are trying to determine what facts are in dispute that will require further investigation. If you immediately suspend the target, the target may not believe that you have not already made your final decision and he may refuse to cooperate at that point in time. Therefore, unless confronted with a direct question about whether the target will be suspended, it is best to conduct the interview first and, as part of your closing, inform the target that he need not report to work until the investigation is concluded. If the target does confront you immediately, you should not lie, but inform the target that you believe it will aid the investigation if the target is not at work while it is being conducted. It will be important to reassure the target that no decision has been reached and that his being sent home is being done solely to provide an atmosphere to conduct a more prompt and effective investigation.

You should also consider whether the suspension will make matters in the workplace better or worse. If the target is well liked and respected by many employees and the complainant has a history of making complaints, some of which have merit and others that do not, you may do more harm to the investigation by removing a popular manager when you must talk to those who support him.

Once you inform any employee that she or he will be sent home during an investigation, you must be prepared to offer your reasons for your actions and to respond to questions from other employees. The employee being sent home will usually ask what other employees will be told, if they ask about the individual's absence, and you must be prepared to tell the employee how you will respond. So, how do you respond? To the employee being sent home, you should explain it is to protect the individual against retaliation and to ensure a more effective investigation. It may also result in a quicker investigation. To employees who ask about another's absence, you should indicate the employee's absence is related to personal reasons. If employees push for more information, you can explain that just as you do not discuss the questioning employee's business with others, you will not discuss someone else's business with other employees either. Although other employees involved in the investigation will suspect that the employee has been sent home because of the investigation, it is not necessary to offer any information other than it relates to a personal matter.

There may be situations where it is necessary to inform other employees about the suspension prior to informing the employee being sent home. This situation commonly occurs when it is necessary to remove the individual's access to computer programs and networks. For instance, if it will be necessary to review documents and e-mails stored on an employee's computer, you will want to limit the employee's access, from both home and work, to that computer and network. Therefore, you may need to have someone disable the employee's access while you are interviewing the employee and before you inform the employee of the suspension. In that case, it is important that the IT people with whom you deal understand the confidential nature of your request and that failure to maintain that confidentiality will result in immediately disciplinary action. While it is not always desirable to involve other employees, it is far worse to delay these actions and provide the employee enough time to destroy any facts or evidence.

Any employee being sent home will want to know the terms, such as whether she will be paid, when she can return, and what she can or cannot do during that time period. There generally is no legal requirement to pay employees sent home during investigations, but it makes business sense to do so. If you send someone home without pay, it will probably be perceived both as a disciplinary action and as a final decision. If the employee believes her fate is sealed, she may take the time off work to consult an attorney and threaten or begin legal action before you have even completed your investigation. If the employee is not losing any pay or benefits, the employee usually perceives the investigation will be fair and the employee may believe she will be vindicated. Although these perceptions are usually not correct, they may provide motivation for an employee's actions while not at work.

If the employee is an exempt employee under the Fair Labor Standards Act, it may be necessary to pay the employee for an entire week in which any work is performed. Contact your legal counsel before suspending an exempt employee without pay to determine whether that is lawful or not.

One thing you need to stress is that just because the employee is not at work, you still expect the employee to cooperate with the investigation and not interfere with or contact other employees during the investigation. It is also important that if the employee is the target of the investigation that she understand it is improper for her to contact the complainant and that doing so will result in disciplinary action, independent of the results of the investigation. "Do-it-yourself" investigations should never be tolerated.

Another item you must consider is whether the meeting with an employee being sent home could turn out to be violent. In today's day and age, workplace violence is not uncommon and can be deadly. If you have any concern that violence may result, you should contact a local security company or your local police department for advice. You may also want to contact your lawyer to determine if a formal risk assessment should be conducted.

If you determine there is a possibility of violence, you may wish to hire a security official to be nearby in the event the situation does turn violent. Or you may want to put the local police station on notice that a potentially violent situation may occur. Violence does not occur frequently, but you must be prepared for those few situations in which it does occur and be prepared to stop a violent employee as quickly as possible.

Once an employee is suspended, confirm the suspension in writing, specifically identifying what is being investigated, whether the employee will receive pay and benefits during the suspension, how long you expect the investigation to last, that the employee should contact you with any questions or additional information, what is expected of the employee during the suspension and the consequences of not meeting those expectations. When you indicate how long you expect the investigation to last, do not make promises that you will have a final decision by a specific date. Rather, you should indicate what your expectations are for the time it will take to conduct the investigation. The memo should be given to any employee sent home during an investigation, whether the employee is the complainant, the target, or a witness. A sample memo follows:

MEMORANDUM

TO: Sammy Smith

FROM: Polly Personnel

DATE: August 15, 2004

RE: Suspension

Pursuant to our meeting today, you will be suspended from employment beginning today in order to permit the Company to conduct an investigation into allegations of financial improprieties in your department. We stress that the investigation is in its initial stages and that no conclusions have been reached regarding what may have happened, whether you or anyone else may be at fault, and whether disciplinary action is warranted.

While you are suspended, you will continue to receive full pay and benefits, but you will not be expected to perform any duties and you will not be permitted in the workplace. It is expected that it will take approximately 10 days to 2 weeks to complete the investigation. If additional time is needed for the investigation, you will be informed of how much additional time we believe may be necessary. We will schedule a meeting with your when the investigation has been completed.

If you learn any additional information you believe may be helpful to the Company in conducting the investigation or you have any questions, you should direct them only to the undersigned.

During your suspension, you are not to contact any other employees about the investigation, or otherwise interfere with or disrupt the investigation being conducted by the Company. If you do take any of these actions, you will be subject to disciplinary action, up to an including termination, regardless of and independent from the outcome of the investigation.

____

Polly Personnel

____

Received this ___ day of August, 2004.

____

Sammy Smith

CHAPTER 8

ANALYZING THE RESULTS

Now that the investigation is complete, it is time to gather all your notes and documents and analyze what you have learned in order to make a good faith determination of what occurred. In analyzing what you have gathered, you should not ignore common sense and your experiences. And, it is critical that you not be afraid to reach a conclusion because you are afraid you might reach the wrong conclusion. Remember, if your investigation was properly conducted, all you need to do is reach a good faith, reasonable conclusion as to what occurred.

In analyzing the results, you will be trying to resolve the factual disputes that were identified at the beginning of, and possibly during, the investigation. Be careful not to jump to ultimate conclusions. For example, what if you determine that an employee did make one racist comment, showed others one racist cartoon on a computer, and told racist jokes on two or three occasions to four employees, all over the course of a three-month period? Some investigators would make one conclusion — that racial harassment occurred. But did it? In order to have a racially hostile environment, the harassment must be so severe and pervasive as to prevent the individual from achieving equal employment in the workplace. A few isolated incidents in a short period of time generally are not sufficient to constitute such harassment. If, however, an investigator determines that harassment occurred, it might be difficult to convince a jury that while inappropriate, the comments did not rise to the level necessary to create a harassing environment under the law. There should be no doubt, however, that the incidents should be found to violate company policy, dictating disciplinary action to be appropriate. Therefore, it would be appropriate to conclude that the incidents occurred and that such incidents were in violation of the company policy. Whether or not there is a legal issue should not come into play in analyzing the results. If you have a question about the legality of the actions you determine occurred, consult your legal counsel before making those conclusions part of your analysis.

After you have assessed the credibility of your witnesses, you will have made certain assumptions on who to believe or how much to believe of what an individual said. Once you have made those determinations, you should also analyze whether the issue was raised in a timely manner and if not, why not? Was the complaining employee afraid of being denied a promotion, if the target remained in a decision-making role? Did the supervisor repeatedly threaten and retaliate against employees who complained to human resources? You should have gathered at least some information that will help you explain any delay that may have occurred.

You will also want to consider whether you learned of other similar types of behavior that occurred in the past. If the other similar actions were not reported in the past, why were they not reported? The most common situation in sexual harassment cases involves supervisors and managers who assume no one could be offended by their actions and those assumptions turned out to be incorrect.

You will also want to consider whether you uncovered any facts that would indicate an individual's motivation for lying or covering up some things while admitting others. You may also consider whether an individual's stated justification for any actions he or she admits to doing make any sense. Reviewing your notes, determine whether either the complainant or target told you something you later learned could not be true. That may help you determine whether something actually occurred or not. Again, use your common sense.

You should also focus on the timeline. If you drafted your questions and conducted your interviews in such a way as to get a chronological understanding of what occurred, compare the stories you received with your timeline. Big holes or inconsistencies may become more apparent that way. And, it may help you identify other evidence you should gather to resolve any outstanding disputes. For example, if there is a question about whether an individual was at work on a specific day, you can look at that employee's attendance records, expense reports, or calendar to help you determine what did occur.

Once you decide what happened, resolve the factual disputes, and reach your conclusions of the issues at the heart of the investigation, your task is not over. You now need to make a recommendation of what should occur based upon your conclusion on what happened.

CHAPTER 9

MAKING A RECOMMENDATION

Now that you have resolved the factual disputes, what action, if any, should be taken? Unfortunately, that determination rarely belongs to human resources. In most companies, human resources takes control and ownership of the investigation, but management makes and takes control of the final decision as to what, if any, action to take. It is important to understand whether you are making a recommendation or making the decision. If you are making a recommendation, it is important to coordinate with the appropriate members and management, and perhaps your legal counsel, to avoid creating additional problems if your recommendation is not accepted.

For example, assume you determined that the senior vice president of business development, who recently had a religious conversion, has violated company policy repeatedly by requiring employees to profess their faith in God and to participate in weekly prayer meetings. He has also made it clear, verbally and in e-mails, that those who do not believe in Jesus will not survive long in his organization and should immediately consider employment elsewhere. That same senior vice president, however, has also single-handedly been responsible for the company's turn around and subsequent success with his ability to identify new revenue possibilities and joint ventures. The worst situation an investigator can be put in is to write a memo condemning the senior vice president and strongly recommending that termination is the only appropriate remedy, only to be told that there is no way the company would consider terminating that individual regardless of what he does because without him there would be no company. The investigator's memo will be strong evidence against the company that it made a good faith determination that there were enough incidents to constitute religious harassment, but the company unlawfully failed to take appropriate action to prevent the harassment from occurring.

It could be even worse if the complaining employee takes no further action, but subsequent complainants do and their lawyer can demonstrate the company was well aware of the senior vice president's actions and made a conscious decision to allow him to continue to engage in harassing behavior.

So, what is the investigator to do? This is a situation in which coordination with your legal counsel is critical. As discussed in detail in Chapter 11, there are conversations you have with your attorney that are considered privileged, that are protected from others learning about what was said. If the investigator approaches the attorney with the problem before issuing the recommendation, the attorney can also discuss the legal aspects of the investigation and the legal risks associated with taking or not taking specific actions with the appropriate management personnel. That type of coordination can prevent opposite conclusions being reached by different organizations within the company. You should determine before making any recommendations whether this type of coordination through legal counsel is advisable or desirable.

Now that you have determined what happened, you should recommend whether or what type of action is appropriate, based upon your resolution of the factual disputes. Usually the first inquiry is whether the actions constituted a violation of any company rules or regulations. If there were violations, a determination should be made as to how serious the violations were. Once that determination is made, past practice should be reviewed to decide what disciplinary actions have been issued in the past for similar violations. Being consistent is important in defending discrimination charges, and it helps demonstrate that you took appropriate action based upon your investigation results.

Once you determine what would be appropriate under company rules and regulations, you should also consider whether there are any local, state, or federal rules or statutes that require you take any specific actions. For example, if sexual harassment exists, the employer's legal obligations are to take action necessary to ensure it stops. If you have any questions as to what your legal obligations are or if the action you want to take pursuant to the company's past practice is sufficient, contact your legal counsel.

Another factor that may be relevant is how long the employee has been with your company. If the employee has been there a long time and has no history of other discipline, that fact is usually considered to be a mitigating factor that can be used to take a less drastic disciplinary action. Even if the employee has had some disciplinary problems in the past, you should look at the types of infractions for which the employee was previously disciplined. If the employee's past problems all related to being tardy for work, that may not be relevant to the instant recommendation. If, however, the employee has previously been disciplined for similar violations, it may justify more severe disciplinary actions.

Finally, you should consider whether there are any other factors that might justify strict or more lenient disciplinary action. If you have an employee who violates a policy against cohabitating with an employee under his or her supervision, and that employee is the one who wrote the policy, that could justify more severe disciplinary action.

In issuing any type of disciplinary action, it is important to identify what you hope to accomplish by issuing discipline. Do you want to modify an employee's behavior or eliminate the problem and/or employee? Once you have identified the goal, you can identify the different ways to achieve these goals. For each different way you identify, you should consider whether the action would indeed serve to accomplish your goal.

There are innumerable actions you can take against employees. Or, you may take no action based upon the results of the investigation. The most common actions are to place the employee on a step of the progressive discipline program, such as verbal warning, written warning, suspension, probation, or termination. It is also possible, however, to use other methods to achieve your goals. Assume your investigation demonstrated the employee showed insensitivity to cultural differences of employees. You may have also concluded the offending employee was completely unaware of how offensive his actions were. In such a case, warning the employee against such behavior will probably not accomplish your goal of eliminating the behavior. Rather, it will probably take some training for the employee to understand how and why his actions are offensive to help him avoid them in the future. You may also find that it is not just one employee who requires some training, but an entire work group or department.

You may also want to take action that removes an employee from a certain work area, such as a transfer or demotion. Or, you may want a different way of punishing the employee, such as a salary reduction or loss of privileges. Again, it is important that you identify the goal of any actions and to match the two. You should not feel constrained to follow only the options in your progressive discipline system, as there may be more than one way to solve a problem in an effective manner.

Once you determine what to recommend, you should prepare an investigation report. This document will serve as a summary of your entire investigation and, if the investigation was done correctly, anyone reading your summary should reach the same conclusion that you reached before reading what your conclusion is.

The report should begin with a background section that will include information about the complainant and target, summary of the complaint, date the investigation started and ended, the name of the investigator, name and dates of people interviewed, when the final recommendation was made, and a summary statement of the facts. If the investigation was not triggered by an employee complaint, the background section should indicate how information was received that triggered the investigation. The background section should also refer to any documents generated at the beginning of the investigation, such as confirmatory memo to complaining party or suspension notice.

The second section of the report should identify and either summarize or quote applicable company rules and regulations. The third section is a summary of the key factual findings that were made, and it should also include how the facts were analyzed, noting any conflicting or inconsistent information, how the credibility of witnesses was assessed, and why the complainant and target were or were not believed. This fact section should not contain your conclusions, just the facts you collected, whether by document or witness interview.

The fourth section will contain your conclusions. That will include how you resolved any factual disputes, whether there were any company policies or procedures that apply and the bottom-line conclusion, such as that inappropriate comments were made in violation of the company policy. If there were issues not resolved, those should be identified in this section. What should not be included are any conversations you had with legal counsel concerning coordination, if the investigator is not the decision maker. This section should be objective and neutral, and if well written, the reader will reach the same conclusion as the writer. If the investigator is also the decision maker, the conclusion section can also include what the decision was and when it was implemented. If the investigator is not the decision maker, the conclusion section should only contain the investigator's recommendation.

INVESTIGATION REPORT

PREPARED BY: Polly Personnel

DATE: October 2, 2004

RE: Complaint concerning missing entry fees

I. Background

On September 20, 2004, Mark Money reported to his department manager Rob Ruler that he believed his co-worker Jonathan Joker was responsible for the theft of entrance fees. Rob reported Mark's comments to me.

Mark saw Jonathan in work early one morning placing something in the basket where patrons toss coins to enter the facility. When he looked into the basket later, he could not see anything. When Mark asked Jonathan about it, Jonathan told him to "mind his own business." When Mark asked why, Jonathan told him to "shut up or he'd get hurt." Two weeks later Mark heard there were money shortages from the entry booths that could not be explained. A few days later, Mark saw Jonathan leaving work with what looked like a sock that made clinking sounds.

On September 22, 2004, I spoke to Mark and began an investigation that continued until October 1, 2004. Mark agreed that he thought I could fairly and objectively conduct the investigation. After that interview, I prepared a memo to Mark summarizing our meeting. On September 23, I interviewed Jonathan. On the 24th and 25th, I interviewed the other four employees who worked the entry booths and collected fees, Mary Maybe, Jeff Jolly, Candy Sweet and Nick Nasty. The following day, I interviewed Rob. After the interviews were conducted, for four days the employees were observed during the last half hour of their shift and until they left the premises.

On October 1, 2004, an analysis of the investigation was conducted and termination of Jonathan and Mary Maybe was determined to be appropriate. They were terminated later that afternoon.

II. Application of Company Rules

The policy that applied to this situation is the Rule 12, Theft of Company Property.

III. Analysis

1. In the interviews with all employees, they admitted they only handle money if necessary to give change to patrons and that they must deposit the correct fee in the basket for the patron in order for the gate to open to allow the patron to enter the facility. Jonathan was the only employee who knew how the baskets and gates worked as he worked in maintenance when he joined the company.

2. Jonathan had a history of being the first one at work. He usually left last or with Mary.

3. A review of the maintenance logs showed Mary frequently had problems at the end of her shift that required other employees to help her with her booth. Jonathan did not help Mary with these problems.

4. In the interviews with Jonathan and Mary, they said Mark was a poor performer and that he was upset because Mary dated Jonathan and would not go out with Mark, although he had asked her several times.

5. Nick, Jeff, and Candy all reported seeing Jonathan with an old sweat sock that was stretched out of shape. None asked why he carried it around. They all confirmed that at the end of many shifts, they would help Mary with her booth, while Jonathan closed up his. He never helped Mary. Jonathan was always at work first, but no one knew why he came in early or why he stayed late.

6. Nick thinks Mark is interested in Mary as he likes to talk to her, but he has never heard Mark ask Mary out. Nick said Mark was a good worker.

7. During the observations in the last week of September, on one night Mary did have problems and Mark, Nick, Candy, and Jeff all tried to help her. While the other employees were helping Mary, Jonathan appeared to open the back of the coin basket from inside his booth. He had a lump under his shirt when he left his booth. Jonathan waited for Mary and they walked to Jonathan's car. In the car, Jonathan was observed pulling something out of his shirt and giving it to Mary who laughed and smiled.

8. The collections balanced every day during the investigation except the day when Mary was observed having problems requiring the attention of the other employees. On that day, although Jonathan's booth registered collections, there were none in the collection basket. There was a hook made of a paperclip in the collection basket and cotton elasticized threads hanging from the paperclip.

IV. Conclusion

Based upon the investigation, the observations conducted and analysis, it was determined that Jonathan was inserting a sock into his collection basket so that fees deposited by patrons would pass the trigger to open the gate, and be deposited into the sock instead of the collection basket. Mary would create a diversion at the end of the day to allow Jonathan to retrieve the sock, which was filled with coins from his collection basket, by using the maintenance door inside the booth to access the collection basket.

Theft of company property has always resulted in termination of the employee. After discussing the appropriate discipline with Rob, it was determined that both Jonathan and Mary should be terminated under Rule 12. They were terminated on October 1, 2004.

The report will become part of the investigative file. This file should now contain the investigator's notes, any documents reviewed, any documents given to or received from an employee, including memos, and final disciplinary notices. The only documents that should go into an employee's file is the disciplinary notice, although it is appropriate for the notice to refer to the investigation that was conducted. Even though the investigation is concluded, however, does not mean they should become "public." The file should remain as confidential as possible and should be maintained by the investigator. Remember, it can be several years before a complaint or lawsuit is filed concerning an investigation, so it is best to maintain everything in one file in a safe place.

CHAPTER 10

IMPLEMENTING THE FINAL DECISION

Once the investigation is complete and the recommendations and decisions have been made, those decisions must be implemented and the complainant and target informed of the results of the investigation. While the investigator's primary responsibility is to see that the investigation is conducted fairly and effectively, it may also be necessary for the investigator to wrap up the investigation as well, even if the investigator does not make the final decision. Remember, investigations are collaborative in nature, often requiring coordination with several departments other than human resources.

If the investigator is not the decision maker, the recommendation should be discussed with the decision maker prior to preparation of the investigation report in order to fully discuss any points of disagreement and, if necessary, to involve legal counsel. Once the decision is made on what action will be taken, the next decision is who will implement the decision. The answer to that question will depend upon how things are done in your organization. If the direct supervisor is the one who usually issues discipline, the direct supervisor should also issue the discipline resulting from the investigation. If, however, the human resources department issues discipline, that procedure should not change. If no disciplinary action will be issued to the target, then it is appropriate for the investigator to meet with the target to inform him of the results.

Regardless of who meets with the target to issue any disciplinary action, that individual should be prepared to explain why the decision was reached. This conversation should not be used to debate or rehash the investigation or to give the employee an opportunity to change your mind. The employee must understand the decision has been made and while you are prepared to discuss certain aspects with the employee and answer questions, the decision is not open to debate and will not change.

If the employee is not terminated, there will be additional questions you should anticipate, including whether the results of the investigation will be placed in the employee's personnel file. The employee should understand that all disciplinary actions go into the personnel file, including this action, but that no other documents from the investigation, unless there was a suspension notice, will be placed in the employee's file.

If the investigation involved many employees, you will probably be asked who else in the company is going to be told about what happened. As with the inquisitive employee who wants to know why someone is not at work, you should limit your response and indicate that you do not discuss one's employee's record with another. And, you should assure the target that nothing else will be said.

Occasionally, someone will actually ask, "How will this affect my future at the company?" You should never make any promises, if confronted with such a question; just respond that it will depend upon how the employee behaves from this point forward and that the employee will be expected to comply with all policies and procedures or be subject to further disciplinary action.

If the target is being disciplined but will continue to work with or around the complaining party, you may have to explain, again, that retaliation will not be tolerated and that the employee will be expected to follow company rules and regulations when dealing with all employees. If the target asks for a transfer, you should offer him the same rights any other employee has when requesting a transfer.

If disciplinary action is issued, you should follow the same procedures you follow to issue discipline to any employee. If you have a specific disciplinary form that you use, use it in this instance as well. Some trainers recommend giving a memorandum to the target detailing the reasons why you reached the conclusions you did and informing the target of the basis for the action taken. Such memos, however, can confuse juries and make them revisit every decision you made during the investigation. It is better to have the jury focus on the investigative report, rather than on a disciplinary notice that will be challenged every way possible by the target.

In some cases, the results of the investigation will be inconclusive or will demonstrate disciplinary action is not warranted. This conclusion should be shared with the target. If there is no basis upon which to believe one party over the other and no basis for action, it may still be appropriate to remind the target of the policy at issue and that violations may lead to disciplinary action. In addition, depending upon the nature of the complaint and individuals involved, it may be wise to remind the target that you believe the complaint was made in good faith and that no retaliation will be tolerated.

Meeting with the target is not the final step to complete the process — someone needs to meet with the complaining employee. This is normally done by the investigator, not the employee's supervisor, unless there will be discipline issued for bringing a fraudulent complaint. Unlike other employees, the complainant should be provided information concerning what the result of the investigation was and why it was reached. You should tell the complainant what the conclusion was and why you reached that conclusion. You should also inform the complainant of what action is being taken as a result of those conclusions. The complainant may disagree with your decision and you may expect disagreement before the meeting occurs. The worst way to deal with this issue is not to say anything. While the complainant may disagree with your decision, not informing her of what the decision is, will ensure she never considers the matter to have been finalized and closed.

If the target will remain in the workplace, you should remind the complainant that retaliation will not be tolerated and that if any occurs it should be reported to you immediately. Even though you are sharing your results with the complainant, the complainant must understand that the confidentiality requirements still apply.

The complainant must not discuss anything you have discussed with other employees and that if she does so, disciplinary action may follow.

It is not necessary to prepare a written report or memorandum to the complainant. As with written results to the target, if the complainant disagrees with anything in your memorandum to her, each disagreement may be magnified in front of the jury and the issue of whether you made a good faith determination may give way to whether all of your conclusions were right.

The meeting with the complainant may be one that not just reports the results of the investigation, but also disciplines the complainant for bringing a fraudulent complaint. In that case, the same procedures for determining who to issue the discipline and what forms to use that apply to the target will also apply to the complainant.

CHAPTER 11

LEGAL ISSUES

Unfortunately, given the litigious nature of today's society, and the relative lack of penalties against those who bring frivolous and meritless claims, investigators must always be aware of potential legal pitfalls that may be encountered during and after an investigation. If you are thorough, reasonable, and treat all those involved in the investigation in the manner you would like to be treated, you can generally avoid liability for actions taken during an investigation. That does not mean, however, that you avoid ever being sued. If you conduct your investigation appropriately, however, you may be able to have a suit challenging your investigation dismissed without the necessity of a trial. This Chapter is designed to point out the most common types of challenges to investigations and what you should know in order to avoid liability. And remember, challenges may be brought based upon things you say and do after the investigation has been completed and after an employee has been terminated. Just because the investigation is over and the appropriate action has been taken does not mean you should abandon the confidentiality requirements imposed during the investigation.

A. Third-party investigators

Depending upon who the target of the investigation is, the type of complaint raised, or the availability of local management, you may find it necessary to use a third party to conduct the investigation. Of course, anyone you hire should be well versed in how to conduct effective investigations. It is not uncommon for companies to look to their labor lawyers to conduct the investigation. The biggest danger in using your lawyer, however, is that you risk losing any privilege you have with regard to conversations with your lawyer and your lawyer may become a fact witness.

In *Harding v. Dana Transport, Inc.*,[1] the company asked its lawyer to investigation sexual harassment complaints filed with the New Jersey Division on Civil Rights and to draft an appropriate sexual harassment policy. The investigation was conducted and the attorney concluded that no sexual harassment occurred. A position statement was submitted to the Division and a fact-finding conference was held. Consistent with the way most employers defend against these types of complaints, the company relied upon its investigation that found no evidence of harassment. When the Division attempted to learn about interviews the lawyer conducted with the different witnesses, the company asserted those conversations were protected by the attorney-client privilege.

The federal court, however, disagreed, finding that once the company asserted as its defense the thoroughness and reasonableness of its investigation, it had waived its right to assert the attorney-client privilege. The waiver included not only the interviews, but also any and all documents prepared by the attorney. Other courts have reached similar conclusions.

If you have a good relationship with your employment counsel and you would want that counsel to represent you in any litigation that may ensue, you should find someone else to conduct the investigation. Otherwise, your lawyer could become a witness and you will be forced to find other counsel to represent you. Given the number of organizations that employ human resource specialists and lawyers to conduct investigations, it would be wiser to hire one of these companies, if you need an outside investigator. Regardless of whom you use as a third-party investigator, ensure that they are aware of their obligations under the Fair and Accurate Credit Transactions Act ("FACTA"), as discussed in section C, below.

B. Attorney-client privilege

The attorney-client privilege allows clients to have frank and open discussions with their lawyers without the risk of having to

---

1. 914 F. Supp. 1084 (D.N.J. 1996).

divulge the contents of those conversations to others. If you have a confidential conversation with your attorney and limit dissemination of that conversation only to those who have a need to know, you can usually protect those conversations by invoking the attorney-client privilege.

Some people believe that so long as a lawyer is hired to look over the investigator's shoulder, everything discovered in the investigation is privileged. That, however, is a dangerous misconception. In many cases, as in the *Dana Transport* situation, you will want to rely upon what you learned in your investigation to defend your actions. There will be situations during the investigation where it will be appropriate to discuss matters with your lawyer and to protect those conversations from disclosure.

While you cannot protect facts learned in an investigation from disclosure, you can protect advice you received from your attorney concerning those facts. If your lawyer does not raise the issue of whether the conversation will be privileged, you should not be afraid to do so. The lawyer may ask you to do certain things in order to preserve that privilege depending upon the applicable state law. In general, you should address your communications to the attorney, whether verbal or in writing. It is also advisable to label documents as "Privileged and Confidential." Finally, you should not discuss your conversation or share any documents you send to the attorney with others who do not have a need to know about the communication. State laws differ as to how they define individuals with whom the information can be shared without losing the privilege. If there is any doubt in your mind as to with whom you can share the information, ask your lawyer. If you share the information too widely, that can destroy the privilege and require you to disclose your communication.

C. FACTA

In 1999, in an opinion letter written by a staff attorney at the Federal Trade Commission ("FTC"), employment lawyers were shocked to learn the FTC was taking the position that any investigations of workplace misconduct conducted by third parties were subject to all the requirements of the Fair Credit Reporting Act. This opinion was based upon an interpretation of the 1996 amendment to the Act. The FTC found such third parties, including lawyers, to be "consumer reporting agencies" within the definition contained in the statute. Under the statute, employers using third-party investigators would be required to inform the target of the investigation, disclose the scope and nature of the investigation, obtain the target's permission before preparing a report, and provide a waiting period before any adverse action could be taken. It is difficult to conceive that Congress intended the same requirements that applied to obtaining credit histories to apply to workplace investigations. Unlike credit reporting agencies, there has never been any evidence that employers make numerous, repeated mistakes when investigating employees.

This situation was corrected in December 2003, when President Bush signed the Fair and Accurate Credit Transactions Act ("FACTA"). FACTA took effect on March 31, 2004. Section 611 of the Act specifically exempted investigations concerning suspected workplace misconduct from the definition of "consumer report." In order to satisfy the exemption, the following conditions must exist: the communication is made to the company in connection with a workplace investigation; the investigation concerns either suspected misconduct in the workplace, or compliance with applicable laws, rules of a self-regulatory organization, or written company policies; the communication does not involve credit worthiness, credit standing or credit capacity; and dissemination of the communication is limited to the company or its agents, a governmental agency, a regulatory agency, as required by law, or under any other FTC procedure. If the investigation meets these requirements, the provisions of the 1996 amendment will not apply.

There is, however, a requirement that the company provide a summary report from the third-party investigator to any employee against whom the employer takes adverse action as a result of the investigation. It is not necessary to identify the witnesses interviewed or specific statements made by any witnesses. There is no longer a requirement that the report be provided before any adverse action can be taken. It can now be provided after the employee has learned of the adverse action. If action is taken against an employee that is not based upon the investigation conducted by the third party, then no summary need be provided to the employee.

D. Defamation

One of the most common claims stemming from investigations is defamation. That is, a false statement was made about an employee to another, without privilege to do so, that resulted in harm to the employee. In harassment cases, these claims may be filed not only against the company, but against the complaining parties as well. There are two common defenses to defamation claims — first, that the statement made was true, and second, that the employer had a qualified privilege to repeat the information.

In order to foster open communication, a privilege exists to make or repeat a statement when both parties to the communication have an interest in the subject. It is under this doctrine that employer statements during investigations are privileged. Unlike statements made in judicial proceedings, which are absolutely privileged, the privilege application to investigation is only a qualified one. If an individual acts with malice in making the statement, the privilege can be lost. Malice can exist when the employer acts in bad faith, knew the statements to be false yet made the statements anyway, or is reckless or excessive in publishing the information to others. *See, e.g., Barthelmes v. Martineau.*[2] To avoid a finding of malice, it is important to limit discussing your investigations and the allegations with those who may have relevant information and that you do not condone employees' spreading false statements either during or after the investigation is concluded.

2. 11 Mass. L. Rep. 617 (2000).

Although failure to conduct an investigation or failure to conduct a thorough investigation is not, in and of itself, malice, an employee allegedly defamed during an investigation will be able to delve into the specifics of the investigation, or lack thereof, in order to try to prove malice.[3] Therefore, you should ensure that you do not engage in any actions that may invite a defamation action or convince a jury that you acted with malice during an investigation. It is important that you exercise care when discussing matters that could harm an employee's reputation.

Another type of defamation action that may exist is self-compelled defamation. In those cases, the plaintiff alleges that because of the investigation and its results, the plaintiff is required to defame himself by repeating the results of the investigation when seeking subsequent employment. The basis for permitting such claims is that it is foreseeable that an individual, given the circumstances, will necessarily have to repeat the defamatory statements. Former employees making this claim usually allege they had to reveal their former employer's reason for discharge in an interview and that the reason was defamatory. Although such claims are recognized in many states, the qualified privilege that protects the employer from defamation during the investigation process can also continue to protect the employer against self-compelled defamation.[4]

E. Negligent investigation

One of the most common, and least successful, negligence claims is for negligent investigation. The plaintiff usually alleges there are things the employer should have done that would have demonstrated the employer's conclusion was incorrect and that because the employer was negligent in conducting the investigation, the plaintiff was wrongfully harmed.

---

3. *See* Boyd v. Nationwide Mut. Ins. Co., 208 F.3d 406 (2d Cir. 2000).

4. *See, e.g.,* Theisen v. Covenant Med. Ctr., 636 N.W.2d 74 (Iowa 2001).

Fortunately for employers, in states where the employment at will doctrine prevails, courts have been reluctant to recognize a cause of action for negligent investigation. This refusal is based upon the theory that if an employer can discharge an employee for any reason or no reason, it does not make sense to hold an employer liable for terminating an employee for not conducting a thorough investigation, when the employer need not have any reason at all for its actions.[5]

---

5. *See* Texas Farm Bureau Mut. Ins. Cos. v. Sears, 84 S.W.3d 604, 608-09 (Tex. 2000), noting the following: Walt v. State, 751 P.2d 1345, 1351 n.9 (Alaska 1988) (holding that there is no negligent-investigation claim "in a public employer-employee context"); Chellsen v. Pena, 857 P.2d 472, 476-77 (Colo. Ct. App. 1992) (refusing to recognize a claim for negligent breach of a contractual duty to examine an employee's record); Morris v. Hartford Courant Co., 200 Conn. 676, 513 A.2d 66, 68 (Conn. 1986) (declining to recognize a negligent-investigation claim); Theisen v. Covenant Med. Ctr., Inc., 636 N.W.2d 74, 82 (Iowa 2001) (rejecting a negligent-investigation claim because it "goes to the heart of the employer's decision-making process" and would "create an exception swallowing the rule of at-will employment"); Bagwell v. Peninsula Reg'l Med. Ctr., 106 Md. App. 470, 665 A.2d 297, 320-21 (Md. Ct. Spec. App. 1995) (holding that an employee does not have a negligent-investigation claim, in part, because of the at-will employment relationship); Ferrett v. General Motors Corp., 438 Mich. 235, 475 N.W.2d 243, 246 (1991) (concluding there is no duty to evaluate or correctly evaluate an employee before termination); Lambert v. Morehouse, 68 Wn. App. 500, 843 P.2d 1116, 1118-19 (Wash. Ct. App. 1993) ("We conclude that Washington courts have not and should not recognize a cause of action for negligent investigation."); Wilder v. Cody Country Chamber of Commerce, 868 P.2d 211, 222 (Wyo. 1994) (holding that there is no claim for negligent investigation); *see also* Vice v. Conoco, Inc., 150 F.3d 1286, 1292 (10th Cir. 1998) (declining, under Oklahoma law, to recognize the negligent-investigation tort when the plaintiff alleges that the employer did not investigate harassment claims); Johnson v. Delchamps, Inc., 897 F.2d 808, 811 (5th Cir. 1990) (holding that, under Louisiana law, an employer may terminate an at-will employee even if the reason for termination was based on incorrect or carelessly gathered information); Rice v. Comtek Mfg. of Oregon, Inc., 766 F. Supp. 1544, 1549 (D. Or. 1990) (stating that, under Oregon law, there is no duty to investigate an employee's conduct before termination); Gossage v. Little Caesar Enters., Inc., 698 F. Supp. 160, 161, 163 (S.D. Ind. 1988) (concluding that, under

These holdings do not mean, however, that the plaintiff's attorney will not continue to assert the claims hoping to find judges willing to recognize such causes of action. Even if the cause of action has not been recognized in your state, you do not want to be the test case. Employers who insist on defending extreme and unreasonable actions may end up making bad law for all the other employers in their state. Therefore, do not assume you will remain immune from negligent investigation claims if your conduct your investigations in a slapdash manner resulting in considerable harm to one who is wrongfully accused.

If there is an actual or implied contract only to discharge an employee "for cause," there is a greater danger of losing a case challenging the method and scope of your investigation. In *Cotran v. Rollins Hudig Hall Int'l, Inc.*,[6] the California Supreme Court held the employer's burden was to demonstrate that it "reasonably believed" the misconduct occurred and that it acted "fairly" based upon that information. The factors the court indicated should be examined included whether the employer acted in good faith, whether the decision was made after an appropriate investigation, and whether the employer reasonably believed the misconduct occurred. It was not necessary for the employer to prove it occurred, it just had to prove a reasonable belief existed.

Indiana law, there is no negligence claim for the employer's conduct of a polygraph and voice-stress test that led to termination); Butler v. Westinghouse Elec. Corp., 690 F. Supp. 424, 430 (D. Md. 1987) (holding that, under Maryland law, an employer has no duty to investigate the employee's alleged violation of company policy); *but see* Chamberlain v. Bissell Inc., 547 F. Supp. 1067, 1080-81 (W.D. Mich. 1982) (recognizing a duty of ordinary care in performing contractual obligations, including conducting an annual performance review); Kizer v. Semitool, Inc., 251 Mont. 199, 824 P.2d 229, 235-36 (Mont. 1992) (explaining that although Montana does not generally recognize a claim for negligent termination, negligently failing to investigate an employee before discharge states a "separate and distinct" claim).

6. 17 Cal. 4th 93 (1998).

In determining whether an investigation was "appropriate," the courts will look at whether the investigator knew how to conduct investigations, who was interviewed, the types of questions asked, whether confidentiality was maintained, whether witnesses were asked to stay in touch if additional information was discovered, whether the target was informed of the allegations and given adequate opportunity to respond, and what the basis of the ultimate decision was. Where an employer "listened to both sides" and could articulate a basis to prove a reasonable belief existed, there was no liability based upon the conduct of the investigation.[7] An employer will have a more difficult time defending the investigation, however, if the complaints are not documented, not all parties are interviewed, there is no follow up on new information, and there was no attempt to monitor the ongoing interactions between the employees involved.[8] If an employee is not employed "at-will," you should be especially vigilant in ensuring your investigation is prompt, thorough, and reasonable.

F. False Imprisonment

While some witnesses may seem uncooperative, there will be those who simply refuse to participate in an interview. In those cases, it is important that you do not restrain the employee, physically or with threats, or otherwise prevent an employee from leaving whenever the employee desires. False imprisonment claims are made when an employee is willfully detained without consent and without the authority of law.[9] If an employee is threatened in such a way that the employee cannot exercise his free will to leave, a false imprisonment claim may exist. If an investigator is physically larger than the employee, blocks the employee's way out, and uses

---

7. Silva v. Lucky Stores, Inc., 65 Cal. App. 4th 256 (1998)

8. Carrisales v. Dep't of Corrections, 65 Cal. App. 4th 1492 (1998).

9. *See, e.g.*, Randall's Food Markets, Inc. v. Johnson, 891 S.W.2d 640, 644 (Tex. 1995).

size and tone of voice to scare the employee into consenting to the interview, the consent may be held to be invalid. While an employer does have the right to investigate misconduct in its workplace, it does not have the right to detain an employee as part of the investigation. Therefore, you should always allow an employee to leave. You may inform the employee of the consequences of leaving, such as continuing the investigation without input from the target, or disciplining other witnesses; however, you should not take any other actions designed to prevent the witness from leaving.

G. Representation during the interview

To the surprise of most employers, under a National Labor Relations Board case, certain nonunion employees have the right to have a co-worker attend the investigatory interview with them. The Supreme Court of the United States recognized the right of employees in a union bargaining unit to have a union representative present when the employee was subjected to an interview that the employee reasonably believes could lead to disciplinary action.[10] In 2001, the Court of Appeals for the District of Columbia Circuit affirmed the Board's decision to extend that right to nonunion, nonsupervisory employees.[11] The Supreme Court refused to hear the appeal of that decision. Employers who do not follow it, risk a charge being filed against them with the Board and the finding that they committed an unfair labor practice.

It is important that employers understand the scope of what is and what is not required under this decision. First, they only apply to investigatory interviews where the employee reasonably believes he could be subject to disciplinary action. Therefore, to witnesses who are not the target of the investigation the decision generally will not apply. If a witness insists upon representation, it

---

10. NLRB v. J. Weingarten, Inc., 420 U.S. 251 (1975).

11. Epilepsy Foundation of Northeast Ohio v. NLRB, 268 F.3d 1095 (D.C. Cir. 2001), *cert. denied*, 536 U.S. 904 (2002).

should be denied until and unless something comes up in the interview that would indicate that there is a reasonable basis upon which to think disciplinary action may follow.

If an employee is entitled to have a co-worker present, but does not ask for one at the beginning of the interview, the right has not been waived. At any point during the interview, the witness may ask that a co-worker be allowed to attend. Once the co-worker is located, the employee is entitled to a description of what is being investigated and to conduct a short consultation with the co-worker before the interview begins or continues. Although supervisors are not entitled to have a representative present, an hourly employee may select a supervisor as his or her representative during an interview. Employees are not permitted, however, to have legal counsel present as their representative. Only employees covered by the National Labor Relations Act, which excludes supervisors, are entitled to representation.

Some employees may name co-workers who they know are not present. You do not need to delay the interview for more than a reasonable time. If the requested co-worker is not at work, or is on an extended vacation, you need only inform the employee that co-worker is unavailable and that he or she must select another.

Even though an employee may be entitled to have a co-worker present, an employer is not required to inform the employee of that right or ask the employee if he or she would like a co-worker present. Nor do you have to permit the co-worker to interfere with the interview. The co-worker's presence is to assist the employee, which implies an obligation to cooperate.

An employer always has the right not to conduct the interview if the employee asks that a co-worker be present. You can offer the employee the right to continue the interview without the co-worker or not going through with the interview. The problem with this approach is that you will miss hearing one side of the story and you may not be able to conduct a thorough investigation.

Once a decision to take adverse action has been made, the employee is not entitled to have a co-worker present during the meeting when the employee learns his fate. The right only extends to interviews that may result in disciplinary action.

This decision greatly complicated an employer's ability to conduct workplace investigations. Until and unless another Court of Appeals refuses to enforce a Board decision requiring such representation, there will be no basis for Supreme Court review. The only other hope for employers is that as the make-up of the Board changes, the new members will realize the error in the decision and reverse it so that it only applies in unionized environments.

H. Medical records

If an investigation involves an employee's medical condition, such as if it involves whether an appropriate accommodation was provided, there are additional requirements that will apply to any medical records you obtain during an investigation. Under both the Americans with Disabilities Act and the Family and Medical Leave Act, medical records must be kept confidential and separate from other employee records. The only exceptions to the confidentiality requirements are for supervisors or managers who need to know in order to provide the accommodation, for first aid, or safety reasons, or for governmental investigations. Of course, if an employee requests an accommodation, the employer has the right to ask for appropriate medical documentation of the need for an accommodation and to share that information with third parties consulted on what accommodations are available. The ability to use the information in determining whether an accommodation is appropriate, however, does not mean the information loses its confidentiality. Once the issue is settled, the statutory provisions will apply. Therefore, if medical records are involved, you should maintain two investigative files, one for medical records, the other for everything else gathered during your investigation.

I. Privacy

Being ever creative, plaintiff's lawyers continue to look for other bases upon which to challenge investigations or the methods used to gather information. One area in which there has been an expansion of rights and obligations, caused in part by technological advances, is privacy law. When there appear to be few other method of challenging an investigation, some creative lawyers assert the methods used to gather information violated an employee's right to privacy.

The courts, however, have not been as willing to adopt such theories. Most privacy actions are based upon the creation of a reasonable expectation of privacy. One way to defeat those claims is to ensure employees understand that there is no such expectation with respect to company equipment or resources. In *Fraser v. National Mutual Ins.*,[12] the court held there was no violation of the Electronic Communications Act when the employer opened and read e-mails stored on its system. The e-mails in question were reviewed without the employee's knowledge and contained disparaging comments about the company sent to outsiders. Despite the plaintiff's arguments, the court was not persuaded that opening e-mails stored on the company's server constituted an unlawful interception of a communication under the law. The court also noted that service providers were free to access e-mails stored on their systems at will.

In order to make clear to employees that there is no expectation of privacy with respect to e-mails, voice mails, or use of company-provided equipment; you should put a policy into place that informs employees of this fact. A sample policy follows:

12. 352 F.3d 107 (3d Cir. 2003).

USE OF COMPANY EQUIPMENT AND SEARCHES

E-mail and voice mail

The Company provides e-mail and voice mail systems for employees to communicate with one another. In order to protect the confidentiality of communications, each employee has a distinct password to access his or her mailbox. All employees should be aware, however, that each department manager has the ability to access the mailboxes of all employees in his or her department.

The Company does not have a policy of monitoring e-mail or voice mail messages or reviewing them for content before they are transmitted to the recipient. Nevertheless, employees must realize that these are business systems, and not personal communications networks or bulletin boards. Accordingly, employees will be expected to maintain the same degree of professionalism expected in all business communications when using e-mail and voice mail.

In the event the Company receives information that an employee is abusing the system or is sending harassing, damaging, or defamatory messages, an investigation will be conducted and the employee will be informed at the beginning of the investigation. If any employee has abused the right to use e-mail or voice mail, he or she may be disciplined in any manner consistent with the progressive discipline policy.

Complaints about information sent over the system or about messages sent to a specific employee should be brought to the supervisor's attention. Whenever possible, employees should obtain a hard copy of the message about which they wish to complain. The supervisor and the human resources department will handle all complaints discreetly.

Internet access

The Company also provides Internet access to employees. The Internet is a vast resource that allows employees to research customers, techniques, and general information with the stroke of a few keys. The Company believes it is important for employees to use the Internet as a tool to help them perform their jobs better and more efficiently. Therefore, the Company has established an Internet account that may be accessed by employees.

Employees will be provided with passwords and addresses to enable them to use the Internet account. Employees must be aware, however, that usage of the Internet is subject to the same code of conduct that applies to all other actions in the workplace. Use of the Company Internet account in a manner that violates any Company rules or regulations constitutes grounds for disciplinary action, up to and including discharge.

In order to protect Company information, employees must not share their passwords with any other individuals, including other employees or outsiders. Nor is it appropriate to attempt to subvert network security either by accessing the Internet without using your password or by seeking to discover other passwords to gain access. Violation of these principles will result in discontinuance of your right to use the Company Internet account and may lead to further disciplinary action.

Employees should remember that they are representatives of the Company when using the Company Internet account. Accordingly, they are expected to act and to communicate professionally on the Internet. Employees are not to engage in any commercial or illegal activities while using the Company Internet account.

As owner of the Internet account, the Company will have access to a log of all usage, including a list of employees who have used the Internet and the sites they visited. The Company will monitor this usage from time to time, and employees found to be abusing usage or using the Internet inappropriately will be subject to disciplinary action.

The Company will not tolerate employees downloading or copying information from the Internet that may be viewed as harassing or defamatory. Internet communications are subject to the harassment policy and employees suspected of violating the policy will be subject to investigation and possible disciplinary action.

Searches

The Company reserves the right to engage in any lawful method of investigation when the property of customer, employees, or the Company is missing, or when the Company suspects that information or equipment is being removed from the premises. One method the Company may use is to search any and all containers, employee belongings, or vehicles on Company property. Employees must understand that anything they bring onto the property is subject to this policy that includes but is not limited to purses, briefcases, computer bags, shopping bags, backpacks, and lunch boxes. The Company also reserves the right to search any vehicles brought onto Company property and any place on Company property where property may be stored, including desks and lockers.

Employees will be asked to sign a form consenting to the search. By consenting to the search, however, employees are not excused from complying with all Company rules and regulations and may be subject to disciplinary action, up to and including termination, if the employee is found to be in possession of property not belonging to the employee or information the employee is not authorized to have or to remove from the premises.

An employee who does not consent to a search will be subject to immediate disciplinary action, up to and including termination.

J. Intentional Infliction of emotional distress

Another set of claims with which employers must deal are intentional infliction of emotional distress claims. Intentional infliction claims are valid only if the plaintiff can demonstrate that the actions taken by the employer were extreme and outrageous, beyond all bounds of decency, that were intended to, and caused, severe emotional distress in the plaintiff.[13] Intentional infliction claims are very difficult to prove. It is not sufficient that the complained of behavior be rude or boorish. Nor is behavior that constitutes unlawful harassment necessarily sufficient, standing alone, to

---

13. Texas Farm Bur. Mut. Ins. Cos. v. Sears, 84 S.W.3d 604 (Tex. 2002).

also constitute intentional infliction. There must be something else, such as planting a forged check in a plaintiff's purse, demoting a senior office to janitor, or similar actions. The best practical advice to follow to avoid intentional infliction claims is to treat others like you want to be treated. Do not call someone a thief, as you escort them out of the building after completing a theft investigation, and do not demean or belittle employees in front of others. If you remember and follow the golden rule you will go a long way toward protecting your company against liability.

CHAPTER 12

TRAINING

CASE STUDY

It's a beautiful early spring day at 5:30 p.m., when Susie, an administrative employee from the accounting department, nervously peeks into your office and asks if you will be around later this week because she might want to talk to you about how her boss treats her. She can't talk much now because her ride is waiting.

QUESTION 1. What do you do?

a) Ask what she means by "might" want to talk to you?

b) Tell her the weather has been so nice that you will probably be leaving early the rest of the week and will not have time for her.

c) Tell her you will be in all week and to call you whenever she is ready to talk.

d) Invite her into your office, ask a few questions, and set an appointment to talk to her further.

Susie arrives at your office about half an hour late for your appointment with her. She's looking around as if to see who is watching her go into your office.

QUESTION 2. What do you say?

a) Do you realize you're half an hour late? That will limit our time together.

b) I'm sorry Susie. We have to reschedule.

c) Hi Susie. It's nice to see you again. Please take a seat.

d) I hope you can talk quickly, as it's almost quitting time.

Susie sits down and you ask her what it was about her boss that she wanted to discuss with you. Susie tells you her boss, Greg, makes her very uncomfortable by the way he treats her. When you ask her what she means, she just says, "He doesn't treat me the way you should in an office."

QUESTION 3. What type of questions would you ask Susie at this point?

In response to your questions, Susie tells you the following:

- She's very uncomfortable with the way that Greg looks at her. She says he gives her lewd looks, like he is undressing her with his eyes.
- She had some questions about the new health insurance plan, and Greg said, "Come to lunch with me, and I'll explain the new changes."
- When she came in with a cold one day, Greg said, "That's what happens when you sleep naked."
- One night when she was working late, and she was stretching her neck because it was stiff, Greg came up behind her and started massaging her neck. He stopped when she told him to stop.
- Greg rubs the necks of lots of women, including Chris and Molly, women who worked for him for a long time.
- A friend sent Greg a dirty e-card via e-mail, and Susie heard Greg laughing about the card with Jeff and Mark.
- Jeff, Mark, and Greg make jokes about how Chris and Molly dress and their hairstyles.

- Greg and Jeff joke about employees "going commando" at work.
- One day, some paper got stuck in the copy machine and Susie could not get it out of the machine. She was bent over, pulling on the paper when Greg came up behind her and rubbed up against her as he leaned over and removed the paper that was stuck.

QUESTION 4. Is an investigation warranted? If so, what additional information do you need from Susie?

QUESTION 5. Now that you have determined an investigation is warranted, how will you conduct the investigation?

QUESTION 6. Draft some of the questions you would ask Greg when you interview him.

You call in Greg for his interview, and he is very jovial and relaxed. He does not have any idea why you have asked to meet with him. When you tell him there have been allegations made that he has behaved inappropriately toward some females in the company, he stiffens up, then bellows at you, "Who said that?" Before you can draw a breath, he stands up and says, "I've never done anything wrong. You get whoever it is in here immediately and make her confront me if she thinks it's true! I'll show her!"

QUESTION 7. How should you respond to Greg?

When you talk to Greg, you learn that he has been with the company for over seventeen years and that Chris and Molly have worked for him that entire time. Jeff transferred in from another office about six or seven years ago, and he and Greg have become friends, socializing every once in a while and playing golf together. Greg hired Mark about four years ago and has had no problems with him. Susie transferred into Greg's department a couple of years ago from the advertising department. Greg heard through the grapevine that Susie thought her old boss was after her, so she asked for the transfer. Her old boss, Robbie, was hired at the company the same time as Greg; he's been married for over thirty years and has three kids, one of whom is disabled and will always live at home with Robbie. Robbie retired the same time Susie transferred into Greg's department.

Greg admits that he uses "going commando" in the office to refer to men who do not wear underwear. He says the joke came up based on a beer commercial he saw in which women ask a confident guy walking through the bar if he's "going commando." He and Jeff saw the commercial together, thought it was funny, and now it is a joke between them. They also joke about it with Mark. Greg denies asking any women about "going commando," but does not know if any women were around when he, Mark, and Jeff were joking around.

Greg's brother got a prescription for Viagra, so friends starting sending his brother dirty jokes and pictures about Viagra, which his brother sent to Greg. Greg does not remember showing them to anyone or keeping them on his computer. He usually just reads them and deletes them. He might have mentioned something to Jeff and Mark when they are just engaging in "man talk."

Chris was a massage therapist before she came to work for the company, and she taught Greg and Molly how to do massages. They frequently massage each other's necks and backs at work. He remembers rubbing Susie's neck on several occasions. One time, she said that was enough, and he just thought it was because her neck was feeling better, not because she wanted it to stop. He stopped when she said that was enough.

He has never heard or made any comments at work about anyone sleeping in the nude. Greg does call Chris and Molly "big hairs" because they wear their hair teased with lots of hairspray. He started using the term after Chris and Molly referred to themselves as "big hairs." He also jokes about their clothing because they like to wear western-style clothes, so they can go "boot scootin'" after work. He says that means going country and western dancing.

The copier in their department jams all the time. He doesn't really know how to fix it, but has had to yank out stacks of paper when the girls cannot remove what is stuck. Sometimes it takes two people to pull out a stack of paper. He thinks he has helped all the employees clear paper jams.

Greg could not recall anything particular about how Susie dressed or if he said anything to her. She usually keeps to herself, even eating lunch at her desk instead of joining the others. He likes to take the employees in his department out to lunch on a regular basis to find out what is going on, but Susie has never joined them. Greg is sure he has asked her to lunch because he usually asks all the employees when he decides to take anyone to lunch or when he wants to just talk to an employee to see how things are going.

Greg suggested someone talk to Darlie, who used to work in advertising and was friends with Susie. Darlie and Susie are no longer friends, and Greg thinks it is because Darlie got a job that Susie wanted just before she transferred. Susie does not seem to get along with many women in the workplace. She does not talk much to Chris and Molly and seems unhappy that because of their seniority with the company, they get assignments Susie would like to have.

QUESTION 8. Pursuant to your investigation plan, you have interviews set up with Jeff, Mark, Chris, and Molly. Does Greg's interview indicate you should do anything else as part of your investigation?

Your review of the personnel files did not reveal anything relevant or significant. After interviewing Jeff, Chris, Molly, Mark, and Darlie, you learn the following:

From Jeff: Jeff, Mark, and Greg frequently joke about going commando. They all like to talk about sex, but usually only in Greg's office. Greg has shared some e-mails with Jeff, but Jeff cannot remember any specifics, but there was not anything shocking or disgusting. Jeff does not think any of the females were ever around when he, Mark, and Greg are joking around or talking about sex.

From Chris: Chris was more than happy to tell you how wonderful her department was and what an important part of the team she was. She also told you she was very "plugged in" to what was going on in the department, so she is glad you are talking to her. She offers to talk to you again if other things come up on which you need some clarification.

Chris admits that she was a massage therapist and that she taught everyone in the department how to massage each other's necks, except Susie. Since she had these special skills, she thought it was nice of her to teach her co-workers these same skills, although they clearly were not as accomplished at it as Chris was, since Chris was an actual therapist. She says Greg and she frequently give each other hugs, but it is not offensive, and she likes it. Greg also hugs Molly a lot and Molly does not complain.

Chris has never seen him touch Susie. She says Susie does not interact well with others and she just seems uptight and ready to jump on people for everything little thing. Chris works with Susie sometimes and says her work is okay, but she is always looking for the easy way out of doing things. Chris needs to spend more time with Susie to see if Susie can do the work, but Chris has been too busy. Chris is certain that once she can teach Susie her way of doing things, Susie will be a good employee. Chris taught Molly how to do things, and Molly is a good employee, so it should be the same with Susie. Susie thinks Chris and Molly get the easy jobs, and she is not happy about that. Chris said the jobs are not easier; it is just that after being with the company so long, she has a way of doing things that is very efficient.

Chris has heard Jeff and Greg talk about going commando. Chris says Greg has a healthy sex drive, and he is not too old to still be interested in sex. She does not really remember Greg saying anything inappropriate at work. She knows Greg outside of work. She and her husband socialize with Greg and his wife, exchange birthday and Christmas gifts and have a warm relationship. She thinks anyone who thinks Greg acts inappropriately needs to grow up, because he does not do anything wrong.

From Molly: Molly initially did not want to discuss anything about her department, and it took a lot of reassuring to get her to open up. She said she and Chris had worked for Greg for a very long time and that because of that they were more casual than most employees. She does not socialize with Greg, Jeff, or Mark outside of work, but she does socialize a lot with Chris. She said Chris thought massaging each other was a good idea, and a long time ago she taught Molly and Greg how to massage the neck. Molly was uncomfortable with it at first, but realized it was not that bad. She prefers Chris to massage her neck, and she tries to avoid letting Greg do it, as she feels uncomfortable when he is that close to her.

She did confirm that she and Chris dress up to go dancing after work and that they call themselves the "big hair girls." It doesn't bother her when Greg calls them that, as well. She says she is aware that Greg, Jeff, and Mark have private discussions, but she does not listen to what they talk about. She says that is their business, not hers. She could not recall any specific things she might have overheard or phrases they might have used.

The copy machine breaks a lot, and it does usually take two people to clear a jam. Greg likes to help because there is close contact when two people clear a jam. Molly usually just waits until Chris is around to get help rather than tell anyone else there is a jam.

Molly said that Susie keeps to herself, is quiet, and does not seem very friendly, but she does her job okay.

Molly stressed that she loved her job, loved where she worked, and would hate to see anything change.

From Mark: Mark did not seem to know what was going on in the department and denied seeing or hearing Greg do anything inappropriate. He says he has heard Susie on the phone using obscene language, and he thinks she is telling dirty jokes when he hears her. He does not think Susie is very competent at her job.

From Darlie: Darlie was very suspicious when you talked to her, and she did not want to answer any questions. When Susie's name was mentioned, however, she immediately complained about Susie and said she was a nasty witch who was jealous about Darlie getting promoted by Robbie. She said Robbie was the best boss she ever had and that anything Susie did was wrong and Susie should have been fired. Darlie said that she and Susie were never friends; she just trusted Susie as a co-worker, and Susie stabbed her in the back by getting jealous of Darlie's new job. Darlie did not offer any other information, as every question was answered with a complaint about Susie. Darlie thinks Robbie just got tired of all the stuff going on at work and decided to retire. She said there was no reason anyone would complain about him.

QUESTION 9. What impressions might you form from these descriptions of the interviews and the information gathered?

QUESTION 10. Is there anything else you want to add to your investigative plan before you analyze the results?

You are able to reach Robbie by phone. He is about to leave town for a month and cannot come in to see you. Robbie tells you that he had been thinking about retiring for about a year, because it was getting harder for his wife to take care of their disabled child by herself everyday. There was an early retirement package available at the time he retired. When asked about Susie, he said that she was a difficult employee to manage. Her work was okay, but she did not communicate well with other employees. She only talked about employees to complain about them. She was very sensitive, and when she got mad at an employee, she would complain about everything they ever did that she did not like. Robbie did not think there was any merit to her complaints, and after she talked about them, they seemed to go away. When Darlie was promoted over Susie, Susie complained to Robbie that he did not treat Susie they way you should treat employees at work. When Robbie asked what she meant, Susie said he showed favoritism to prettier girls, and he talked to them inappropriately. Robbie told Susie that he disagreed and ended the conversation. As far as Robbie knows, Susie never complained about him to his boss or human resources, although she did grumble in the department, making it hard for her to work there. Robbie thinks that was why she transferred. Robbie retired the same time Susie transferred, and he admitted that dealing with Susie made him realize how much he was ready for retirement, which was why he took the package.

QUESTION 11. Write your final investigative report.

ANSWERS

In many instances, there are no right or wrong answers to the questions. How you conduct your investigation is a matter of personal style. This case study is to provide examples of the techniques discussed throughout the book and to help you hone your investigating skills.

QUESTION 1

d) Clearly the first two answers indicate you are not interested in employee complaints (and you probably should not be working in human resources). The third answer, while indicating an openness and willingness to talk, may result in Susie never telling you what happened. Her nervousness about even stopping by your office indicates that she probably had to work to summon the courage to talk to you, so you should take advantage of the situation and see if you can pin down a time to talk to her. By asking just a few questions about her boss, you may be able to determine how urgent it is for you to talk to her. You cannot talk to her for too long as she has someone waiting on her to go home. But, in a few minutes, you can take the opportunity to make Susie feel comfortable with you to ensure she will come back at the agreed upon time.

QUESTION 2

c) Obviously, the other choices demonstrate your impatience with Susie and any problems she might have. You observed Susie was nervous when you first talked to her and knew there was a possibility she might not want to talk. Her concern about being spotted going to human resources demonstrates she is still nervous. Since she has summoned the courage to come back to talk to you, you should simply invite her in and try to make her comfortable.

QUESTION 3

At this point, you still do not know what the real issue is. Although you may be leaning toward thinking a sexual harassment problem exists, do not let your presumptions get in the way of asking the right questions. Some questions you might want to ask include:

- What does Greg do to you that makes you uncomfortable?
- What does Greg do that you do not think is appropriate in an office environment?
- How has he made you feel uncomfortable?
- When does Greg do these things?
- Where does Greg do them to you?
- Do you know why Greg does these things?
- Who else does Greg do this to?
- Has anyone else seen Greg do these things?

QUESTION 4

An investigation is warranted, since you cannot make a determination based solely upon what Susie has told you. You will need more facts to determine whether Greg's conduct occurred and violates any company policies.

You should try to get more information from Susie, such as exactly where and when each of these events occurred, and who was around when each incident occurred. You should also ask Susie again why she thinks Greg would behave this way.

QUESTION 5

The first thing you should do is to ensure that Susie is comfortable with you as the investigator. Assuming she is, you will want to review Susie's and Greg's personnel files to determine if there have been any disputes or issues between them, whether either has been involved in similar complaints or investigations, and if there is an acknowledgement from each that they have read and that they understand the company's sexual harassment policy. Next, you should identify the individuals to interview. Based upon Susie's interview, those should be Greg, Jeff, Mark, Chris, and Molly. There is nothing in the information you received from Susie that would indicate that you will need any expert assistance or that you need to obtain documents from any other source.

QUESTION 6

The first seven questions are examples of broad questions seeking general information. The questions after that are examples of specific questions relating to the allegations raised by Susie. This is not meant to be a comprehensive list of questions, but representative questions designed to help you start developing your own questions.

1. Who do you work with on a daily basis? How long has each been with the Company?
2. Describe to me where the employees' desks are located in your department.
3. How do you get along with the people in your department?
4. Where is the copy machine located in your department?
5. Who do you usually have lunch with? What do other employees in your department do for lunch?
6. Do you ever compliment people? How?
7. Do you receive e-mails from people outside the company? Who? What type of e-mails do they send you?
8. Do you share e-mails you receive from people outside the company with anyone in the company? Who? When?

9. Do you know what "going commando" means? What does it mean to you? Have you ever used it at work? When?
10. Have you ever had to clear a paper jam from the copy machine? How often? Do you remember when? Have you ever helped anyone fix the copy machine? Who?

QUESTION 7

Tell Greg that the purpose of the investigation is to gather facts, not to spark a confrontation. If Greg pushes to know the identification of the complainant, explain that it is not appropriate at this time, as you just want to ask him questions about how he relates to employees. Ensure Greg that no decision has been reached and that you are still in the preliminary fact-finding phase of the investigation and that you hope he will be able to give you facts that will help resolve the issue and identify other individuals who may be able to help.

What you want to do is diffuse the situation, get Greg to understand no determination has been made, and get him comfortable enough to work with you instead of against you.

You will need to tell him who made the complaint and ensure that he does not retaliate against Susie. You can also ask him what questions he would ask Susie and tell him you'll consider them when you talk to her again. These statements should not be made, however, until later in the interview.

QUESTION 8

Greg's interview indicates there are at least three tasks you should add to your task list. The first is to find out what happened when Susie transferred to Greg's department and why Robbie retired. It appears Susie may have made another complaint, and you should find out, if so, whether it was investigated and what the results were. You should also obtain Darlie's personnel file to see what jobs she has held and review Susie's file to see if they ever competed for the same job. Finally, you definitely need to add Darlie to your list of interviewees.

QUESTION 9

With respect to Jeff, he admitted talking about "going commando," talking to Greg about sex, and looking at Greg's e-mails, all of which have a ring of credibility and do not sound like they would be made-up facts.

With respect to Chris, her joy and willingness to participate indicate that she likes the limelight, so anything she told you should be measured against this behavior. She admits teaching people how to massage one another and adds that Greg hugs her and other employees. These facts tend to indicate credibility and that she would not make up those types of things. She also admits Susie does not spend a lot of time with others and is somewhat envious that Chris and Molly get specific tasks she would like to have. Chris's concern that she must train an employee in order for the employee to become a "good employee," indicates she may not be a good judge of Susie's work.

Molly's discomfort may indicate employees need to "get along to go along" in the department. She does not seem to have any problems with Susie's work and is clearly concerned that something may happen to her as a result of talking to you. She indicates there is a special relationship between Chris and Greg that she does not mind, as long as Greg does not bother Molly. Her inability to remember specific conversations indicates she may be trying to cover up something to save her job. Molly confirmed that Greg likes to touch people, although Molly is not as comfortable with it as is Chris, and Molly avoids telling Greg the copier is broken, wanting to work with Chris instead, when there is a jam.

Mark's total denial of knowing or hearing anything does not sound credible, especially since Greg and Jeff have already admitted to talking about sex and laughing about things in the workplace.

Darlie clearly has an ax to grind against Susie, and she seems to think Susie was somehow responsible for Robbie's departure.

You may interpret the interviews differently or come to different conclusions, which is fine. As long as you can reasonably explain the basis for your decisions, you are on the right track.

QUESTION 10

One open item is whether there was any complaint lodged against Robbie. There was nothing in the file, but your interviews seem to indicate something might have occurred. If possible, you should try to contact Robbie to see what happened.

QUESTION 11

There is no right or wrong way to write the report as long as it demonstrates the reasonableness and completeness of your investigation. In this case study, three conclusions are possible: 1) that nothing inappropriate happened; 2) that Greg was engaging in inappropriate behavior by touching his female employees, talking about sex, and looking at and talking about dirty e-mails, and that behavior violated company policy, requiring disciplinary action and possible training; or 3) that the actions Greg engaged in were serious violations of the harassment policy, requiring immediate discharge.

If you role-play this case study, the conclusions reached by those being trained will differ depending upon how those playing the different roles come across. Even if you do not engage in role-playing, different people will read the case study in different ways and come to different conclusions or focus on different aspects. Again, the purpose of this case study was not to get you to reach a specific conclusion. The purpose was to help you think about how to conduct an investigation and provide practice in drafting questions and writing reports. The more investigations you conduct, the easier these tasks will become. And you will realize that no two investigations are ever the same.

POWERPOINT PRESENTATION FOR TRAINING INTERVIEWERS

The following presentation summarizes the concepts set forth throughout the book that can be used to help you train other members of your human resources team or in other departments who will be responsible for conducting investigations of employee complaints. The presentation can be used in conjunction with the case study, or it can be used separately, depending upon the size and sophistication of the group being trained. You can add your own notes to the slides for situations common in your company for illustrative purposes. The training can also be used to familiarize managers and supervisors with the process that is followed when an investigation is conducted and to help them learn when to come to you with disputes.

INVESTIGATING EMPLOYEE COMPLAINTS

A TRAINING PROGRAM FOR INVESTIGATORS

WHY EFFECTIVE INVESTIGATIONS ARE IMPORTANT

- Goals are dispute resolution and litigation avoidance.
- Fact finders will evaluate what an employer knew and what the employer should have known when reviewing investigations and discipline flowing from them.
- Deficiencies in investigations may be fatal to upholding disciplinary actions. Some states allow employees to sue for negligent investigations.
- Should be designed to help you reach a reasonable conclusion.

WHAT MAY TRIGGER AN INVESTIGATION

- Most common—employee complaints.
  - Recognize when duty to investigate is triggered.
  - Do not refuse to act when an employee complains and says, "But I don't want you to do anything about it."
- Customer, vendor, and contractor complaints.
- Above may be anonymous. Don't just ignore.
- Annual policy or statistical reviews.
- Extreme, unexplained changes in behavior.

HOW TO DETERMINE IF AN INVESTIGATION IS WARRANTED

- Investigations only necessary when facts are in dispute.
- If only a misunderstanding is involved, you may be able to resolve on the spot.
- Focus on information provided by the employee
  - Do you need more facts to resolve the problem?
  - Is the issue simple or complex?
  - Are other employees involved?
  - Is this just a single incident or a pattern of incidents?
  - How significant is the issue to your company?

THE INITIAL EMPLOYEE INTERVIEW

- May be planned or unplanned—need to be prepared in any event.
- Set the tone and establish a comfort level.
  - Ask if the employee believes you can be fair and impartial.
  - If employee does not believe you can be objective, do not get defensive. Be creative or find another investigator.
- Identify all the issues.
  - You will need to ask questions to get to the real issues.
  - Take notes so you don't miss anything.
  - Listen long enough to learn what real complaint is.

THE INITIAL EMPLOYEE INTERVIEW (cont.)

- Gather the facts known to the complainant.
  - Ask open-ended questions so the employee gives you facts and doesn't just confirm or deny what you say.
  - Focus on the 5 Ws—what, who, when, where, and why. Keep asking why.
  - Avoid legalese. Ask, "Who was there when this happened?" instead of "Who were the witnesses?"
  - Maintain control of the questioning. The complainant should not be asking the questions.

THE INITIAL EMPLOYEE INTERVIEW (cont.)

- Concluding the interview.
  - Thank the employee and advise of company policy against retaliation for those who make legitimate complaints.
  - Advise employee who will conduct the investigation.
  - Stress and define confidentiality. Indicate employee should not discuss with anyone but you and obtain employee's agreement.
  - Tell employee you will need continued cooperation and may have to talk to the employee again.
  - Stress the company makes the final decision, but ask employee for suggestions on how to resolve.

EMPLOYEE STATEMENT

- Decide if you want employee to write a statement. It should include the following:
  - List of complaints/problems;
  - Facts and dates supporting complaints/problems;
  - Names of people who may have helpful information;
  - Employee's suggestions for gathering information;
  - Employee's signature and date; and
  - Agree on date statement will be turned in to you.

EMPLOYER MEMO

- Determine if you want to provide a confirmatory memo to the employee. If so, it should include the following:
  - Identification of complaints/problems;
  - Facts provided by employee;
  - Who will conduct investigation; and
  - Detail what will be expected of employee as investigation continues.

PLANNING THE INVESTIGATION

- Set up a separate investigations file. Do not maintain investigative notes in personnel files. Be mindful of requirements for medical information.
- Determine if you need legal assistance.
- Determine if you're still the appropriate interviewer.
- Decide how the investigation will be conducted, based on what is being investigated.
- Identify policies and procedures to be copied and reviewed.
- Identify other documents to review, *i.e.*, personnel files, e-mails, expense reports, notes, calendars, diaries.

PLANNING THE INVESTIGATION (cont.)

- Identify the individuals to be interviewed.
  - Interview the target first to help find out what is in dispute, identify other possible witnesses and to help judge witness credibility and may help avoid defamation claims.
  - Consider work schedules and which employees may gossip in setting order of other interviewees.
  - Plan to interview only those necessary to making a determination to stay focused and efficient.
  - Decide whether to use confidentiality acknowledgements and prepare in advance.
  - Ensure a private location in which to conduct interviews.

PLANNING THE INVESTIGATION (cont.)

- Identify any expert assistance, from either inside or outside the company, that will help you gather facts.
- Conduct the investigation as quickly as possible.
  - Don't want memories to fade.
  - Don't want witnesses to become unavailable.
  - Don't want witnesses to become tainted by talking to other witnesses or hearing about investigation through the grapevine.

PLANNING THE INVESTIGATION (cont.)

- Draft your interview questions.
  - Prepare an outline of questions.
  - Try to ask questions in chronological order.
  - Ask broad, open-ended questions, not "yes" or "no" questions.
  - Ask simple, straightforward questions.
  - Save tough and confrontational questions for the end of the interview if possible.

CONDUCTING THE INTERVIEWS

- Most important part of most investigations—and highly subject to attack.
- Anticipate questions and have responses prepared.
- Treat interviewees as you would like to be treated.
- Make interviewee feel at ease.
- Have opening comments ready for each interview.

CONDUCTING THE INTERVIEWS (cont.)

- Special considerations for interviewing the target of the investigation:
  - Identify, in general terms, what you are investigating.
  - Do not let target ask questions or make demands.
  - Stress importance of getting full information from target.
  - If target will not cooperate, inform target the investigation will continue and a determination made without target's input.
  - No confrontation with complainant allowed. Ask target what he would ask complainant.
  - Stress company policy against retaliation when appropriate.

CONDUCTING THE INTERVIEWS (cont.)

- General interview guidelines
  - Explain what is being investigated, the interviewee's role, how you intend to use what you learn.
  - Do not promise the interviewee will not get in trouble for anything revealed during the interview.
  - Do not reveal the identity of other interviewees.
  - Interviewees need to know that no decisions have been made.
  - Explain need to keep the investigation confidential.
  - Explain company policy against retaliation.
  - Explain need to get truthful, accurate facts.
  - Investigation results will not be shared with interviewee.

CONDUCTING THE INTERVIEWS (cont.)

- General interview guidelines (cont.)
  - Stress the importance of the investigation and the need to get truthful and accurate information.
  - You do not want the interviewee's opinion.
  - You do not want the interviewee to speculate about what could have happened.
  - If interviewee refuses to cooperate, explain failure to cooperate could lead to disciplinary action.

CONDUCTING THE INTERVIEWS (cont.)

- Ending the interview
  - Ask if there are other individuals you should talk to.
  - Review critical facts and ask if anything was left out.
  - Reemphasize confidentiality and need to discuss anything related to the investigation with you.
  - Consider reminding the interviewee about policy against retaliation.
  - Answer questions the interviewee may have.

CONDUCTING THE INTERVIEWS (cont.)

- Dealing with difficult witnesses.
  - Total denial—denies each and every thing you mentioned
    - Try to explore motivation
    - Determine if there are other issues
    - Goes to credibility
  - Uncooperative
  - Center of attention
  - Has an ax to grind

TAKING NOTES

- Always retain your original notes—do not plan on rewriting them.
- Notes can be taken during or after an interview.
- Focus on factual observations, not conclusions.
- Supplement your notes with additional observations after the interview has concluded.
- Maintain the confidentiality of notes.

ASSESSING CREDIBILITY

- Several factors will influence how you determine credibility
  - Witness demeanor
    - Body language
    - Changes during interview
    - Reactions to questions
  - Logic and common sense
    - How witnesses stories relate to one another
  - Corroborating evidence
  - Circumstantial evidence

SUSPENDING EMPLOYEES DURING THE INVESTIGATION

- May be necessary to protect other employees or Company property.
  - Allegations of violence of physical assault
  - Allegations of criminal misconduct
  - When necessary to protect property such as claims of embezzlement
- Decide whether to announce before or after investigatory interview with employee.
- Consider the effect on the workplace and investigation.
- Be prepared to tell employee why suspension is necessary.

SUSPENDING EMPLOYEES DURING THE INVESTIGATION (cont.)

- Be prepared to respond to other inquiries as to why employee is not at work.
- Decide on terms of suspension—paid or unpaid?
- Determine if there is a potential for violence and how to respond.
- Confirm terms of suspension with a memo.
  - Issues under investigation
  - Whether paid or unpaid and if benefits accrue
  - How long investigation is expected to last
  - What is expected and consequences of failure to comply

ANALYZING THE RESULTS OF YOUR INVESTIGATION

- Gather all notes and documents to resolve factual disputes.
- Do not avoid reaching a conclusion for fear of reaching the wrong one.
- Do not just look to reach ultimate conclusions and avoid making legal conclusions.
- Consider timeliness of complaint and whether any reasons for delay were uncovered; whether there is a pattern; what motivation or justifications were provided; and how the timeline relates to the interviews.

MAKING A RECOMMENDATION

- Is the investigator making a recommendation or decision?
  - If another department or individual makes the decision, consider coordinating with legal counsel in sensitive situations.
- Factors to consider:
  - Whether company policy violated and severity of violation
  - Actions taken in similar situations
  - Whether there are any legal requirements dictating what action to take
  - The employee's history—longevity, disciplinary history
  - Other relevant factors

MAKING A RECOMMENDATION (cont.)

- What is the goal of taking action—behavior modification or problem elimination?
- Options—match goal with action
  - Use of progressive discipline system
  - Training of individual or groups
  - Transfer, demotion, loss of pay or benefits

MAKING A RECOMMENDATION (cont.)

- Prepare an investigation report containing the following sections:
  - Background information
  - Company rules and regulations effected
  - Analysis
  - Conclusion

IMPLEMENTING THE DECISION

- Determine who will meet with the target if discipline will be issued.
  - Also explain why decision was reached, but don't debate it—the decision won't change.
  - Anticipate questions about what others will be told, whether transfer is appropriate.
  - Confirm retaliation is not appropriate.
  - Use regular forms to issue discipline.

IMPLEMENTING THE DECISION (cont.)

- Meet with the complainant.
  - What conclusion was reached and why.
  - What action, if any, is being taken.
  - Reassure that retaliation will not be tolerated.
  - Confidentiality must continue to be maintained.

POTENTIAL LEGAL ISSUES

- Use of third-party investigators
- Attorney/Client privilege
- FACTA
- Defamation
- Negligent investigation
- False imprisonment
- Representation during interviews
- Medical records
- Privacy
- Intentional infliction of emotional distress

INDEX

Notes

Notes

Notes

Notes

Notes

Notes

Notes

Notes

Notes

Notes

Notes

Notes

Notes

Notes